Callcot. Burt.

MOUNT ARARAT

THE SACRED MOUNTAINS

BY

BETHLEHEM.

J. T. HEADLEY

NEW YORK.

BAKER & SCRIBNER, 36 PARK ROW & 145 NASSAU ST

1847.

THE

SACRED MOUNTAINS.

BY

J. T. HEADLEY

AUTHOR OF NAPOLEON AND HIS MARSHALS, ETC.

ILLUSTRATED.

NEW YORK:
CHARLES SCRIBNER,
124 GRAND STREET.
1862.

TO

MY AGED BELOVED FATHER,

WHO HAS LONG STOOD ON THE HEIGHTS OF ZION

A MESSENGER OF PEACE

AND HERALD OF GOOD TIDINGS TO MEN,

AND WHOSE FEET I KNOW

WILL SOON STAND ON THE "MOUNT OF GOD."

THESE SKETCHES

ARE AFFECTIONATELY INSCRIBED.

PREFACE

The design of the following sketches is to render more familiar and life-like some of the scenes of the Bible. This, I know, is a difficult task, not only from the disposition of men to look at things sacred less naturally than on the common events of life, but from the inability of the writer to find words that shall bring the scenes he would describe, home to the feelings, without shocking his own and the reader's sensibilities by too familiar phrases. Yet, unless they cease to become distant visions to us, we shall never appreciate the displays which God has made of himself to man. The Bible is a book of general principles and outline sketches. To elevate and extend to their full application the former, has been the work of the religious teacher from the time of Christ till now—while the filling up of the latter, has been neglected as impossible or useless. But God has not given us those few bold cutlines of the most thrilling scenes in human history, to have them never completed. In my descriptions, I have endeavored to shun all those things which might be termed mere creations of the fancy, and have confined myself, either to the Bible itself, or to those incidents, which must have occurred, taking human nature to be the same in all ages of the world.

There is one mountain in the list, about which there has been much dispute among writers—I mean Mount Tabor. Every mountain has been more or less the subject of discussion, because its precise locality depends entirely upon tradition. The present Ararat may, or may not, be *the* Ararat on which the ark rested; yet, tradition says it is, and we believe tradition. Neither Sinai or Horeb is so precisely located by the Bible as to furnish no grounds for dispute; and Moriah and Zion have been shifted from spot to spot, to meet the views of travellers. Mount Tabor especially has excited their incredulity, and it is declared impossible that it should be the mount of transfiguration. And yet, at the bottom of all the learning and research expended on this subject, I can find but two reasons against the common belief. One is, that tradition alone declares it to be the mount of transfiguration. But this objection is groundless, or we must give up also the localities of the other mountains, mentioned in the Bible. Ararat itself must cease to be a witness for the deluge. The other reason is, that Mount Tabor was a fortress, and hence could not be chosen by Christ for such an exhibition of himself to the disciples. In the first place, granting the fact, I do not see the force of the argument. Why a mountain, several miles in circumference at the top, could not furnish a removed situation for such a scene, it is difficult to say. If the proximity of men were an objection, one would think that Christ would not have chosen Gethsemane as the place of his agony. But there is no evidence that Tabor, at that time, was occupied as a fortress. Almost from time immemorial, the great plain of Esdraelon had been the meeting-spot of armies, and Tabor furnished a stronghold for whichever party could occupy it. But in times of peace it was often neglected; and that it was in this ruinous state at the period of Christ's transfiguration, is evident from the repairs that were made, and the walls that were built at the commencement of the after-wars between Rome and Jerusalem. At least, there is no other mountain in all this region answering so perfectly to the description—"*an exceeding high mountain apart.*"

The plates are accurate drawings of these mountains, as they now appear, with the exception, that from some of them, mosques have been removed, so as to give them their original form.

As Christ is the beginning and end of all these wonderful displays of divine power, the Star of Bethlehem has been chosen as first in the list of engravings.

CONTENTS.

MOUNT ARARAT.

MOUNT MORIAH.

MOUNT SINAI.

MOUNT HOR.

MOUNT PISGAH.

MOUNT HOREB.

MOUNT CARMEL.

MOUNT LEBANON.

MOUNT ZION.

MOUNT TABOR.

MOUNT OF OLIVES.

MOUNT CALVARY.

THE MOUNT OF GOD.

ILLUSTRATIONS.

ENGRAVED BY BURT.

X

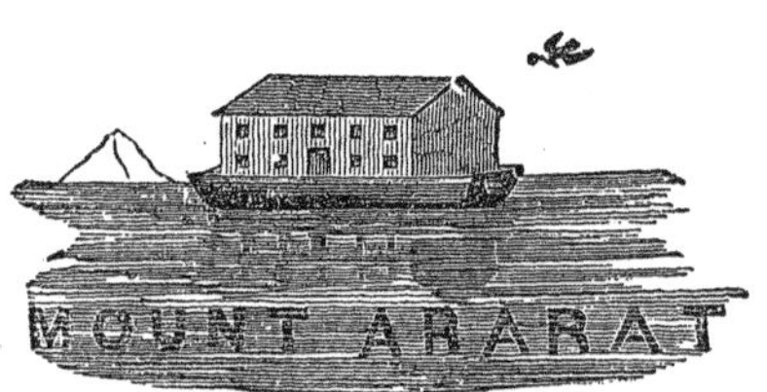

THERE are some mountains standing on this sphere of ours that seem almost conscious beings, and if they *would* but speak, and tell what they have seen and felt, the traveller who pauses at their base would tremble with awe and alarm.

For some good reason, the Deity has usually chosen mountain summits, and those which are isolated, as the theatre on which to make the grandest exhibitions of himself. It may be because those grand and striking features in nature fix the locality of events so that they never can fade from the memory of man. The giving of the law needs no lofty column of stone to commemorate it. Mount Sinai lifts its awful form towards the clouds, a perpetual unwasting monument. God's exhibition of himself to the awe-struck prophet, as he passed by him heralded by the storm, the earthquake and the flame, needs no pyramid to consecrate the spot. Mount Horeb tells where the Almighty dimmed his glory and covered the human face with his fearful hand, so that his brightness might not destroy the being who would gaze on him. The transfiguration of the God-man requires no pillar of brass to arrest the eye and aid the senses as man contemplates the place where the wondrous scene transpired; Mount Tabor is its everlasting memorial. Thus do mountain summits stand the silent yet most eloquent historians of heaven and earth.

Another reason why mountains have been chosen by the Deity for his most solemn revelations, may be that their solitude and far removal from human interruption and the sounds of busy life, render them better fitted for such communications than the plain and the city.

The first in the list of Sacred Mountains is Mount Ararat. The first named summit in human history, it emerges from the flood and lifts its head over the water to look down on all coming generations to the end of time. Whether it was changed in that mighty convulsion which drowned the world, or whether its lofty peak which saw the swelling waters and marked their steady rise remained the same, we know not. At all events, the mountain looked down on the swaying world at its feet, as cities floated from their foundations and came dashing against its sides, and beheld a wilder scene than ever covered a battle-field, as it heard and saw *six generations* shriek and sink together. But whatever may have been its *former* history, it now stands as the only memorial of the flood. Rising like a sugar-loaf from a chaos of peaks, which gleam and glitter in the sun-beams that are reflected from their snowy sides–

overlooking a sea on one side and a desert on the other, it is a grand and striking object in itself, but made still more so by the associations that cluster around its sacred top. It has seldom been profaned by human feet, but there was a time when the sea rolled over it, and mightier waves than ever yet swept the sea thundered high above its crown.

Though the immediate appearance of a flood that should submerge the world was an event that staggered human belief, yet Noah, obedient to the voice of Heaven, began his ark of safety. There is no one who does not lament that there is not a fuller antediluvian history. We merely catch the summits of events, and are told of some half a dozen things that happened, while all the rest is wrapped in impenetrable mystery. We are told that the world was drowned, but the particulars of that terrific scene are left entirely to the imagination. It is only by the declaration of our Lrod, that men were busy at their usual occupations, "eating and drinking, and marrying and giving in marriage, till the flood came and swept them all away," that we get any data by which we can form any true conception of the catastrophe. Yet this short statement is worth every thing, and with it before me, I have sometimes thought I could almost paint the scene. Noah, whose head was whitened by the frosts of six centuries, laid the foundation of his huge vessel on a pleasant day, when all was serene and tranquil. The fields were smiling in verdure before his eyes; the perfumed breezes floated by, and the music of birds and sounds of busy life were about him, when he, by faith alone, laid the first beam of that structure, which was to sail over a buried planet. When men, on enquiring the design of that huge edifice, were told its purpose, they could hardly credit their senses, and Noah, though accounted by all a very upright and respectable man, became a jest for children. As the farmer returned at evening from the fields, and the gay citizen of the town drove past, they christened it "Noah's folly." Those more aged and sober shook their heads wisely, saying, "The old man is mad." Even the workmen engaged upon it laughed as they drove the nails and hewed the plank, yet declared they cared not as long as the foolish old man was able to pay. Still the ark went up, and the day's wonder ceased to be talked about. When it was finished, and curiosity satisfied, it was dismissed from the mind as a passing folly.

Yet I have sometimes wondered what people thought when they saw the beasts of the field and the forest, and fowls of the air, even the venomous serpent and the strong-limbed lion coming in pairs to that ark. This must have staggered them amazingly, and made the ark for a while a fresh topic of conversation.

At length, the patriarch with his family entered—the door was shut in the face of the world, and he sat down on the strength of a single promise to await the issue. That night the sun went down over the green hills beautiful as ever, and the stars came out in the blue sky, and nature breathed long and peacefully. In the morning the sun rose in undimmed splendor and mounted the heavens. Deep within the vast building Noah could hear the muffled sound of life without. The lowing of herds came on his ear, and the song of the husbandman going to his toil, and the rapid roll of carriage wheels as they hurried past, and perhaps the ribald shout and laugh of those who expended their wit on him and his ark together. To say nothing of the improbability of a universal deluge, the idea was preposterous that such a helmless, helpless affair could outride a wrecked world. Thus day after day passed on until a week had gone by, but still the faith of that old man never shook. At length the sky became overcast, and the gentle rain descended—to Noah the beginning of the flood, to the world a welcome shower. The farmer, as he housed his cattle, rejoiced in the refreshing moisture, while the city never checked its gaiety, or the man of wealth his plans. But as the rain continued day after day, and fell faster and fiercer on the drenched earth, and the swollen streams went surging by, men cursed the storm that seemed determined never to break up. The lowlands were deluged; the streams broke over their banks, bearing houses and cattle away on their maddened bosoms. Wealth was destroyed and lives lost, till men talked of ruined fortunes, famine and general desolation; but still it rained on. Week after week it came pouring from the clouds, till it was like one falling sheet of water, and the inhabitants could no longer stir from their doors. The rich valleys that lay along the rivers were flooded, and the peasants sought the eminences around for safety. Yet still the water rose around them, till all through the valleys nothing but little black islands of human beings were seen on the surface. Oh, then what fierce struggles there were for life among them. The mother lifted her infant above her head, while she strove to maintain her uncertain footing in the sweeping waters; the strong crowded off the weak as each sought the highest point; while the living mass slowly crumbled away till the last disappeared and the swift water swept smooth and noiselessly above them all. Men were heard talking of the number of lives lost and the amount of wealth destroyed, declaring that such a flood had not happened in the remembrance of the oldest man. No one yet dreamed of the high grounds being covered, least of all the mountains. To drown the world it must rain till the ocean itself was filled above its level for miles, and so men feared it not, and sought for amusement within doors till the storm should abate. Oh, what scenes of vice and shame and brutality and revelry did that storm witness in the thronged city, and what unhallowed songs mingled in the pauses of the blast that swept by.

But at length another sound was heard

that sent paleness to every cheek, and chained every tongue in mute terror. It was a far distant roar, faint but fearful, yet sounding more distinct and ominous every moment, till it filled all the air. The earth trembled and groaned under it as if an earthquake was on its march, and ever and anon came a crash as if the "ribs of nature" were breaking. Nearer and louder and more terrible it grew, till men forgetting alike their pleasure and their anger, rushed out in the storm, whispering, "The flood! the flood"—and lo, a new sea, the like of which no man had ever seen before, came rolling over the crouching earth. Stretching from horizon to horizon, as far as the eye could reach,—losing itself like a limitless wall in the clouds above, it came pouring its green and massive waters onward, while the continual and rapid crash of falling forests and crushed cities and uptorn mountains, that fell one after another under its awful footsteps, and the successive shrieks that pierced the heavens rising even above the deafening roar of the on-rushing ocean, as city after city and kingdom after kingdom disappeared, made a scene of terror and horror inconceivable, indescribable. "*The fountains of the great deep were broken up.*"

But the last cry of human agony was at length hushed—ocean met ocean in its flow, and the waves swept on without a shore. Oh, what a wreck was there! the wreck of two thousand years, with their cities, cultivated fields and mighty population. Not shivered masts and broken timbers, the remains of some gallant vessel, were seen on that turbulent surface, but the fragments of a crushed and broken world. It was a noble wreck—splendid cities and towers, gorgeous palaces, gay apparel, the accumulated wealth and luxury of twenty centuries strewing the bosom of the deluge, like autumn leaves the surface of some forest stream.

But amid the sudden midnight that had wrapped the earth, and the frenzy of the elements and utter overthrow and chaos of all things, there was one heart that beat as calmly as in sleep: one brow over which no breath of passion or of fear passed: one spirit whose serene trust never shook: for in the solitary ark that lifted to the heaving billows, the aged patriarch knelt in prayer. Amid the surging of that fierce ocean his voice may not have been heard by mortal ear, but the light of faith shone round his aged form, and the moving lip spoke a repose as tranquil as childhood's on the bosom of maternal love The patriarch's God ruled that wild scene and Noah felt his frail vessel quiver in every timber, without one tremor himself. Upborne on the flood, the heaven-protected ark rose over the buried cities and mountains, and floated away on a shoreless deep. Like a single drop of dew this round sphere of ours hung and trembled—a globe of water in mid-heaven. I have often wondered what the conversations were during the long days and nights that lonely ark was riding on the deep. As it rose and fell on the long-protracted swell, massive ruins would go thundering by, whole forests sink and rise with the billows, while ever and anon an uptorn hill, as borne along by the resistless tide it struck a buried mountain, would loom for a moment like some black monster over the waves, then plunge again to the fathomless bottom. Amid this wreck and these sights, the ark sailed on in safety. How often in imagination have I pictured it in the deluge at midnight. To a spectator what an object of interest it would have been. Round the wide earth the light from its solitary window was the only indication of life that remained. One moment it would be seen far up on the crest of the billow, a mere speck of flame amid the limitless darkness that environed it, and then disappear in the gulfs below as if extinguished forever. Thus that gentle light would sink and rise on the breast of the deluge, the last, the only hope of the human race. Helmless, and apparently guideless, its wreck seemed inevitable, but the sea never rolled that could extinguish the star-like beam that told where the ark still floated. Not even the strong wind that the Almighty sent over the water to dry it up, driving it into billows that stormed the heavens, could sink it. Though it shook like a reed in their strong grasp, and floundered through the deep gulfs, it passed unerringly on to the summit of that mountain on which it was to rest; and at length struck ground and ceased its turbulent motion.

Noah waited a week, and then sent forth a raven to explore the deep. Though the waters still swept from mountain to mountain, the myriad carcasses that floated on the surface furnished both food and resting place, and he returned no more. He then sent forth a dove. It darted away from the place of its long confinement, and sped on rapid wing over the flood, now turning this way and now that, looking in vain with its gentle eye for the green earth, and at last turned back towards the ark of rest. The tap of its snowy wing was heard on the window, and the patriarch reached forth his hand and took it in. The fierce pantings of its mottled breast, and its drooping pinions, told too well that the earth gave no place of repose. But the second time it was sent abroad it returned with an olive leaf in its mouth, showing that the earth had risen from its burial and was sprouting again in verdure. Then the patriarch went forth with his family and stood on Mount Ararat, and lo, the earth was at his feet, but how changed. Cut into gorges which showed where the strong currents swept, and piled into ridges, it bore in every part marks of the power that had ravaged it. Noah and his family were alone in the world, and he built an altar there on the top of the solitary mountain, and lifted his voice in prayer, and the Almighty talked with him as "friend talketh with friend," bidding him go forth and occupy the earth. And as the flame of the sacrifice rose from the mountain top bearing the patriarch's prayer heavenward, the promise was given that the earth should never again be swept by a deluge, and lo, God's signet ring appeared in the clouds, arching the man of God, and shown as a warrant that the covenant should never be broken.

Baptized by the flood—consecrated by the altar—illumined by the first fresh rainbow, Mount Ararat stood a *sacred* mountain on the earth.

Turner. Burt.

MOUNT MORIAH.

Mount Moriah stands just without Jerusalem and is now crowned with the mosque of St. Omar, whose entrance has long been forbidden to the Christian, and kept sacred for the followers of Mahomet. It stands where the rude altar of Abraham rose nearly four thousand years ago. The proud city has risen and fallen beside it, the generations of men come and gone, and whole dynasties of kings disappeared one after another, yet there it stands as it stood in the wilderness when it was trodden only by the wild beast of the forest.

The sacrifice of Abraham which consecrated Mount Moriah is to me one of the most touching events in human history. I can never read over the unostentatious, brief account given in the Bible without the profoundest emotions. Knowing that parental feeling and human nature are the same in all ages, my imagination immediately fills up the sketch in all its thrilling details. The shock of the announcement by God—the farewell with Sarah—the three days' lonely journey—the unconscious playfulness of Isaac on the way, and the stern struggle of the father's heart to master its emotions, all rise before me, and I seem to hold my breath in suspense till the voice of the angel breaks the painful spell and the uplifted knife is stayed.

Abraham had long wished and prayed for a son who should inherit his property—bear up his name and transmit it to posterity, until it had become the absorbing thought of his life. Isaac was the child of his old age—his only son—the single link on which every thing rested, and in him were garnered all the love and hopes of his noble heart. But if he was an object of such intense affection and priceless worth to Abraham, what must he have been to Sarah? Oh, who can tell with what absorbing love, what inexpressible fondness, the mother bowed over his cradle and watched his growing strength. Isaac!—that name was to her the embodiment of every thing beautiful and lovely, and his clear laugh never rung out on the morning air without sending a thrill through her bosom almost painful from its intense delight. His voice without the tent would arrest her in the midst of any occupation, and there was no world where her boy was not. But this beautiful scion was to be cut off—this bright young being slain, and the father's hand was to do the deed. So came the command from heaven; and the bolt that then and there crushed through Abraham's heart none but God saw enter. "Take now thy son, thy *only* son

Isaac whom thou lovest,* and get thee into the land of Moriah and offer him there for a burnt-offering on one of the mountains I shall tell thee of." The lightning had fallen and the aged tree was struck though not shattered. The patriarch's fear had come upon him, and he turned to his tent that night with a cloud on his soul the light of faith could scarcely pierce. The voice of his son which had heretofore made his heart leap for joy, now sent a pang through it as if it were the last cry of suffering rather than the call of affection. No sleep visited his eyes that night, yet he kept the fearful tidings to himself and summoned all his energies to meet the terrible trial that awaited him. What! tell the mother that her boy was to be slain and the father to do the deed—that the lamb of her bosom and

* I know that some commentators make Isaac at this time a young man, instead of a child. Whether it is so or not, or whether even the age of twenty-five in that period of longevity was not as young as thirteen now, I shall not discuss. It is enough for me that the Bible calls him "the lad."

the only joy of her heart was to be gashed and marred by the cruel knife and his body burned on a far desolate mountain! that he was to come back no more—his voice to cheer her loneliness no more, but his ashes to be scattered over the bleak hill-side by the winds of heaven! Oh no! the burden was heavy enough already, without taking upon himself the mother's grief. Beside, that boy could never leave the tent in the morning unconscious of his approaching fate, if the mother's farewell was to be a last one. That fatal leave-taking would be a double sacrifice and before the time.

The morning broke clear and beautiful—the asses were saddled and all was ready for departure; yet still Isaac lingered in the tent, covered with the fond caresses of his mother. To part with him a week seemed like losing him an age. But at length she led him forth to the door of the tent, and imprinting a last kiss on his bright young forehead, bade him go. As Abraham saw him approach with half a smile and half a tear on his face, he thought of his own return without him, and the mute despair and crushing agony that would meet him when he should stand speechless and desolate before his wife. Who could answer her inquiries? who still her piercing cries for Isaac her only son? All these thoughts rushed over the patriarch's heart bearing him to the earth, yet his firm soul never betrayed his emotions, and he turned away to meet the struggle before him without faltering or delay. His tent disappeared in the distance, and the last object visible on the plain was the form of Sarah watching them from afar. For three weary days did Abraham journey on, pressed with a single thought, crushed by one over-mastering sorrow, and yet without a heart to sympathize with him. Isaac, on whose pure spirit young hopes lay like morning dew-drops—to whom life was fresh, joyous and radiant, and the earth belted with rainbows—talked ceaselessly of the new objects and scenes that passed before them. But his delights, his innocent enjoyment, brought only a deeper shade on Abraham's brow, and, if he smiled to please his child, it was a smile more painful to behold than his look of sadness. Each answer to his inquiries seemed a heartless deception, and the weary hours a mere prolongation of the mockery of his young affections and desires and joys. And when that son pillowed his head on his bosom at night, and Abraham too desolate to sleep, listened to his calm breathings, methinks his purpose to slay him almost faltered; and, when the morning broke over the landscape, and he watched him still in beauty by his side, the task required of him seemed too great for human strength. But the darker the hour grew, and the more fixed the irrevocable decree, the heavier he leaned on the Omnipotent arm.

After three days' toilsome travel, the mountain at length rose before them, and

Abraham bidding his servants wait his return, took his son and began to ascend its rugged sides. Like the great antitype who bore his own cross up Calvary, Isaac carried the wood for the burnt-offering on his shoulders, while Abraham took the fire and knife in his hand. "So they went both of them together." It requires no vivid imagination to fill up this scene, so slightly sketched in the Bible. Human nature is the same the world over, and as the hour of stern trial approached, Abraham became silent and sad. The fire and knife in his hand, caused him to shudder, for they made what had before been a vision, a passing fact, and he started as the blade glittered in the sunlight, as if he already saw it quivering in his son's bosom. But Isaac, unconscious of the fate before him, continued to talk with all the gaiety and carelessness of boyhood, until, at length, sobered by his father's stern aspect, and the toil of the way together, he too grew silent. As his buoyant spirits subsided, his thoughts naturally turned upon the solemn event that seemed so to absorb and subdue his father. Suddenly it flashed over him that there was no lamb for the offering, and, thinking it must have been forgotten, he turned to his father with an awakened, enquiring look, and exclaimed, "Father, father!" "What, my son," was the half absent reply. "Behold the wood and the fire, but where is the lamb for the offering?" Oh, who can tell the pang that question shot through the father's heart. The tone, the look all showed the very soul of confidence and love, and Abraham staggered under the sudden gush of feeling as if smitten by a blow. But pressing down by a strong effort the emotions that suffocated him, he replied in a faint and tremulous voice: "*My son, God will provide himself a lamb for a burnt-offering.*" This satisfied him, and he lapsed again into silence, though his youthful heart began to tremble before a vague undefined fear of some coming evil.

The mountain breeze as it swept by, had a mournful sound—not a living thing disturbed the solitude, and "so they went both of them together." But when Isaac saw his father begin to bind him, as he had often seen him bind the lamb for sacrifice, and the terrible truth at length flashed on his mind that he was to be slain, who can tell the consternation of his young heart! Oh, who can tell the pleading looks and still more pleading language, and tears with which he prayed his father to spare him! And who can tell the anguish of that paternal heart as it met each sob and agonizing cry with the stern language, "My son, God has chosen thee as the lamb for the burnt-offering." Methinks, as fear gradually yielded to filial obedience, and to the command of heaven, and the moving words, "*my mother, my mother*," died away in indistinct murmurs, that Isaac did not close his eyes against the fatal blow, but opened them instinctively on his father, his only help in that fearful hour, and still watched the glittering blade as it quivered like a serpent's tongue above his bosom, for it was his father who was about to strike. But oh, who nerved the parent's heart in that terrible moment? As his hand put back the clustering ringlets from that fair young forehead, and his glance pierced the depth of those eyes fixed so lovingly yet despairingly on him, who gave steadiness to his arm, and strength to his will, as he bent to the fatal stroke? He who cried, "Abraham, Abraham! spare thy son; Lay not thy hand upon the lad, neither do thou any thing unto him, for now I know that thou fearest God, seeing that thou hast not withheld thy son, thine only son from me." Faith was triumphant—the gold had been tried and found pure, the father tasked to the uttermost and stood, and lo, Isaac bounded from the altar, in all the joy of recovered freedom, and fell on his father's neck in passionate tears. Oh, did ever father and son bend in such overwhelming gratitude before an altar as they, or did the smoke of sacrifice ever go up over two more devoted hearts than then and there went up from the top of Moriah. Faith sublime, unequalled holy faith, consecrated that mountain forever.

Years afterward the temple of Solomon threw the sunbeams upon it, and the children of Israel paid their vows there, but it has no memorial like that of the offering up of Isaac.

Burt.

MOUNT SINAI.

STANDING in the midst of some of the most desolate scenery in the world, Mount Sinai lifts its huge form into the heavens, like some monster slumbering in conscious strength. Its bald and naked summit—its barren and rocky sides, and all its sombre features, correspond perfectly to the surrounding scene. It is a wild and desolate spot, and were there even no associations connected with it, the loneliness and gloom that surround it would arrest the traveller, and cause him to shudder as he pitched his tent under its shadow. But Mount Sinai has associations that render it chief among the Sacred Mountains. The moral, the divine instructions given to man from its summit, are of course the things of chief importance, but as these are always wholly dwelt upon, I speak only of the outward scenes amid which they were imparted. Nor is this without its use; for we, half the time, lose the freshness, I might say the *naturalness*, of much that is said in the Bible, by involving it in a sort of supernatural indefiniteness. We *remove* the persons and the objects, and in doing it lose the power which *familiar* scenes always have over the mind. There can be a no more striking illustration of this truth than in the different effects produced on a congregation by the different manner in which some descriptive scene in the Bible is read. One will read in a strained, monotonous voice, as if *naturalness* betokened too great familiarity with sacred things, and is astonished that men care so little for the reading of the Scriptures. Another, as if he himself were narrating the facts for the first time, and every eye and ear is fixed. If the crucifixion could be made definite as a common murder scene, and the agony in the garden as familiar as the throes and torture of a friend in the extremest agony of human nature, they would not, they *could* not, be read with so little feeling as they are. Said a lawyer to me once, "You Christians lose half the beauty of the Bible by putting your minds into such a strained, solemn attitude the moment you open it. I take it up as I would a law book, and new truths, new beauty, and new sublimity appear on every page." Our *senses* are the inlets to our minds. The Deity acts on this principle when he accompanies all developments of himself with such remarkable outward appearances. Even the Son of God must die amid the throbs of an earthquake, the rending of graves and the blotting out of the sun. The giving of the law, too, was done amid scenes that were designed never to be forgotten.

Behold the white tents of Israel scattered like snow flakes at the base of that treeless, barren mountain. The hum of a mighty population is there, and those flowing tents on which the parting sun is leaving his farewell glories are the only pleasing objects that meet the eye in this dreary region. A solemn hush is on every thing as the moon sails up the heavens, flooding with her gentle light the tented host. Moses has declared that on the third morning the eternal God is to place his feet on that distant mountain top in presence of all the people. Awe-struck and expectant, the sons of Jacob go from tent to tent to speak of this strange event, and then come out and look on the mysterious mountain on which it is to transpire. Unconscious of its high destiny, the distant summit leans against the solemn sky, and nothing there betokens preparation for the stupendous scene.

But at length the morning comes and that vast encampment is filled with the murmur of the moving multitude, all turned anxiously to distant Sinai. And lo! a solitary cloud comes drifting along the morning sky and catches against the top of the mountain. So have I seen a cloud caught by an Alpine summit and held firmly there. But the most vivid impression I ever got of this scene was from Mount Vesuvius. The mysterious cloud it wraps around its own head, concealing the brightness and terror within, always reminded me of the cloud on Sinai. And then the tenacity with which it would cling there. When the midnight heavens were black with tempests, and the sea was one wild waste of waves, and the clouds were dashing like maddened spirits over the sky before the blast—with every flash of lightning that illumined the gloom, I have caught the distant top of Vesuvius with that cloud around its head, moveless as a rock amid the furious blast, while thunder and flame and motion were within. So did the cloud rest on Sinai as the people looked, and suddenly the thunder began to speak from its depths, and the fierce lightning traversed its bosom, gleaming and flashing through every part of it. That cloud was God's pavilion; the thunder was its sentinels, and the lightning the lances' points as they moved round the sacred trust. The commotion which from the first arrested every eye and chained every tongue, grew wilder every moment till the successive claps of thunder were like the explosion of ten thousand cannon shaking the earth. Amid this incessant firing of heaven's artillery, suddenly from out the bosom of that cloud came a single trumpet blast. Not like the thrilling music of a thousand trumpets that herald the shock of cavalry; but one solitary clarion note with no sinking cadence and rising swell, but an infinite sound rising in its ascension power, till the universe was filled with the strain. The incessant thunders that rock the heights cannot drown it, for clearer, fuller, louder, it peals on over the astonished spectators, till their hearts sink away in fear, and nature herself stands awe-struck and trembling before it. And lo! columns of smoke begin to rise fast and furious, from that mysterious cloud, as if a volcano had opened in its bosom, and the pent-up elements were discharging themselves in the upper air; and the steady mountain rocks to and fro on its base, as if in the grasp of an earthquake. "And the smoke thereof ascended as the smoke of a great furnace, and the whole mount quaked greatly."

Amid this rapid roll of thunder, and flashing of lightning, and fiercely ascending volumes of smoke, and convulsive throbs of Sinai, and while that trumpet strain still "waxed louder and louder," Moses led the trembling Israelites forth to the foot of the mountain. Suddenly the uproar ceased, and the thunders hushed their voice, and the last echo of the trumpet died away, and all was still. And from that silent cloud came a voice more fearful than they all—the voice of Jehovah calling Moses up into the mount. The great lawgiver of Israel parted from his people, and with solemn step was seen scaling the rocks and climbing the heights, till at last the cloud received him in its bosom.

The moral law was given, and also the civil code, which men have so learnedly traced to the social compact. The first act in the mighty drama was ended, and Moses was ordered to bring up Aaron and Nadab and Abihu, and seventy of the elders, to worship in the mountain; and God showed himself in his glory to them.

When this strange worship was ended, the voice of Jehovah was again heard issuing from the cloud; but what a change in the mean time had passed over its dark form. A serene and pure radiance began to play around it, quivering like a bright light with its own intensity. Brighter and brighter it grew till the eye turned away dazzled by the sight. Brighter still it gleamed till it seemed a glowing furnace, shooting forth living fire on every side. Its wrathful streaks streamed down the mountain, filling the cavities with deeper gloom, touching every rock and crag with flame, and bathing the white tents in a lurid light. And when the night came on, and darkness wrapped the world, that mountain was one blaze of glory, shedding a strange lustre on the barren scene, and revealing every face and form of that immense host, as if they stood beneath a burning palace,—painting with terrible distinctness, and in lines of fire, the surrounding landscape. The stars went out before its brilliancy, and the moon looked dark in its splendor. For six days and nights did the glory flame on, shedding such a baptism on the wondering camp as was never before witnessed by mortal eye, for "the sight of the glory of the Lord was like a devouring fire on the top of the mount in the eyes of the children of Israel." Little sleep was in the tents of Jacob then, for each one held his breath in awe, wondering what next would nappen in this succession of strange scenes.

At length that voice, before which nature herself seemed to change, again issued from the cloud, calling Moses to a second interview. Taking Joshua with him, he again ascended the hill, and was wrapped from sight "forty days and forty nights."

But as week after week passed by, and there were no farther exhibitions, and Moses did not return, the people passed from idleness into pleasure, and from pleasure into infidelity, and at length emboldened by their own numbers, assembled tumultuously together and demanded another God, saying, "As for this man Moses, who has brought us here, we do not know what has become of him." The golden calf was made, and the intoxicated throng danced around it. What a scene was there! Right at the foot of Sinai, where a month before they had heard the thunders and trumpet and voice, and seen the lightnings and the glory; danced, and shouted, and sung, in bacchanalian frenzy the naked multitude—hailing in boisterous shouts a golden calf as their god! What a contrast to the scene passing on the top of the mountain between Jehovah and Moses!!

In the midst of this wild and blasphemous revel, Moses was seen descending, with thoughtful step, the distant slope, bearing in his arms the tables of the law. At length, as he and Joshua, in serious converse, passed along, they came within hearing of the tumult below. Suddenly stopping, they turned their anxious eyes to the white tents, far, far down in the valley, and Joshua said, "There is fighting in the camp: I hear the sound of battle." But the practiced ear of Moses knew too well the meaning of that confused murmur. "No," said he, "that is not the shout of victors in the pursuit, nor the shriek of the vanquished flying in fear, 'but the noise of them that sing do I hear.'" As he drew near and saw the shameless revel and blasphemous worship, he cast the tables at his feet and rushed into the camp.

The naked throng paled before him as if he had been a messenger of death; the dancing ceased, and the song and deafening shouts were suddenly hushed. Turning neither to the right hand nor the left, he passed, with a brow dark as wrath, to the golden idol, and hurling it into the fire trampled it under foot. Then turning to Aaron, he asked an explanation of this strange scene.

As soon as it was given, he hastened to the gate of the camp, and sending his voice like a trumpet call through the host, cried out, "Whoever is on the Lord's side, let him come to me!" The sons of Levi separated themselves from the crowd and flocked about him. "Seize now, (said he to these,) every man his sword, and go in and out from gate to gate throughout the camp, and slay every man his brother, and every man his companion, and every man his neighbor." Amid the silence that followed were heard sobs and cries of despair; and lo! that terrible band, with drawn swords press into the throng. There is no shout of battle, no cry of anger, though the sword drinks blood at every step. The moan of despair and the sudden death-shriek alone tell where those stern warriors pass. And now, enveloped in the dense mass, the eye can tell where they move only by the flash of dripping swords, as they sweep in angry circles above their heads. Though their hearts bleed at every stroke, and a deeper paleness is on their brow as they sheathe their weapons in their brethrens' bosoms, and the lip quivers before the beseeching look of a once beloved friend, their steadfast hearts must feel no relenting. The dead lie in swaths where they go, and their weary arms droop beneath the protracted slaughter, yet on, on they press, till three thousand corpses cumber the field. Terrible scene—terrible vengeance—but the sword of Divine Justice is ever awful.

Why speak of the after repentance and consecration—of the second ascent into Sinai—of the passing of Jehovah before Moses—

of the still radiance that beamed from his face as he came once more unto the people, until they turned dazzled from his presence. The mighty pageant at length closed—the cloud-column rose from before the tabernacle and moved into the desert; the tents were struck; and the host, headed by that mysterious pillar, in one long column disappeared in the wilderness, and that fearful mountain was left once more alone amid the bleak and barren scenery.

Turned into sapphire by Jehovah's feet, consecrated by his touch, and baptized by the cloud of fire and of glory, Mount Sinai stood the third *Sacred Mountain* on the earth.

Burt.

MOUNT DOR.

XV

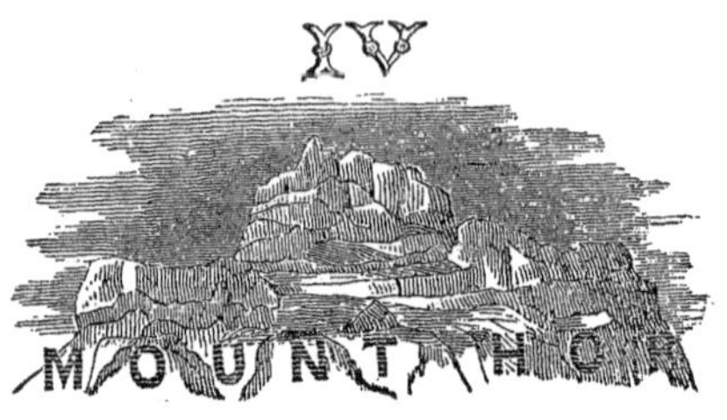

It must have been a grievous offence of which Moses and Aaron were guilty, when commanded to bring water out of the rock for the children of Israel, to have demanded such punishment from heaven as was immediately pronounced. That miracle must have been attended with strange exhibitions of human presumption and rebellion, or God would not have slain the two great leaders of Israel, after all their toils on the very margin of the promised land, and conferred the honor of conducting his people over Jordan, on one whose labors seemed to give him no claim to it. Said God to Moses and Aaron, "Because ye believed me not, to sanctify me in the eyes of the children of Israel, therefore ye shall not bring this congregation into the land which I have given them." Aaron was the first to bow to this stern decree, and died on the top of Mount Hor, while Moses was permitted to feast his eyes on the promised land,—then buried on the summit of Pisgah. These two great leaders in Israel—these wonderful brothers to whom the Gracchi and Horatii of the world are but as dim shadows of men, died on two mountain peaks, making them immortal in history.

Aaron never appears so perfect a character as Moses. He does not seem so much above the follies and prejudices of his age. He was more a man of the times, subject to passing influences and prevailing tastes. Moses, on the contrary, was one of those rare characters in history which seem to live in the past, present, and future. Reverencing the good that has been—understanding the full scope and drift of the present, he at the same time comprehends and lives in the future. Such a man the ardor of hope never beguiles into scorn of the past, nor over-reverence of the present. Like those mountain summits which first catch the sunlight, he rises out of the darkness and prejudice below him, heralding the day that is approaching. Neither does Aaron seem borne up and onward by so lofty a feeling as he. With mind less strong, he lacked also the enthusiasm of his brother. Yet he must have possessed rare gifts to have been chosen the companion and fellow-laborer of Moses in that wondrous deliverance of the children of Israel from Egypt, and in conducting them forty years through the wilderness to the promised land. Much more must he have possessed, an elevation and purity of character far above his fellows, to have been chosen as the founder of the Jewish priesthood—the first to minister at the altar, and to represent a sacerdotal dynasty more glorious and more immortal than the line even of David, or any succession of kings that ever filled a throne.

Chosen by God to stand beside Moses through the night of peril and trouble on which the children of Jacob were entering, he was sent to meet him on his way from the wilderness. Obeying the command, he set out in search of his brother, and lo, they met "*on the Mount of God,*" and kissed each other, and returned together, conversing as they went, to the court of Pharaoh. Who can tell the misgivings and fear of these solitary brothers, standing unprotected by human power before the throne of Pharaoh, and raining on the oppressive monarch the terrible denunciations of heaven? Who has ever repeated their solemn interviews as they retired apart and conversed of the miracles they had performed, and the message of God which daily came to them from heaven? Brave men! day after day they stood between their enslaved brethren and a haughty court, waiting patiently the fulfilment of the promise, still delayed, until at length their efforts were crowned with success, and the thousands of Israel separated themselves from their task-masters, and at midnight moved away from the scene of their degradation and their sufferings. Through all those terrible plagues that desolated Egypt—in the desperate retreat before the thundering chariots of Pharaoh's army—amid the murmuring multitude that clamored against their deliverers who had thus led them forth only to be slaughtered—through the channel of deep waters, while the waves foamed and crested along the high brink that toppled above, Aaron never faltered, but, side by side with his brother, moved firm and steady as the pillar of fire that led them on.

At length he was called forth from the congregation by the voice of God, and ordained High Priest, amid the most solemn ceremonies that ever attended a human anointing, and the sacred robe was put about him, and he stood the mediator between the people and their Maker.

But in the sedition which he planned with Miriam against his brother, he was governed by a spirit of envy and a desire to overthrow him, and exhibited that weakness of character of which I spoke. Yet, doubtless, Miriam was the more guilty of the two, in this shameful conspiracy; for when the Lord suddenly descended in the pillar of cloud, and, with Moses, and Aaron, and Miriam before him, sternly rebuked the erring brother and sister, the latter only was punished. Smitten with leprosy, she emerged from the mysterious cloud that covered the tabernacle, "white as snow." So also in making the golden calf at the bidding of the people, and allowing them to degrade themselves in the eyes of God and man, he showed that he lacked the loftiness of character which made Moses so much feared, and rendered him so utterly incapable of becoming a partner in such folly and wickedness. Still he was made the first High Priest of Israel, and clothed with the richest honors of heaven.

But like Moses, he was not to see Canaan and when the long column of Israel's thou sands stretched across the desert, and wound around the base of Mount Hor, and pitched their tents in its mighty shadow, his work was done and his career ended. Said God to Moses, "Aaron shall be gathered unto his people, for he shall not enter into the land which I have given unto the children of Israel, because ye rebelled against my word at the waters of Meribah. Take Aaron and Eleazar his son, and bring them up unto Mount Hor and strip Aaron of his garments, and put them upon Eleazar his son; and Aaron shall be gathered unto his people and shall die there. And Moses did as the Lord commanded: and they went up into Mount Hor in the sight of all the congregation." Whether the solemn event about to happen to Aaron was made known to the people, and they took a sad farewell of him as they did afterwards of Moses when he went up Nebo, we cannot tell. But from the brief account left us, it is probable that the secret of his death was not divulged to the congregation, and when he and his son, and Moses together, left the camp and began to ascend the solitary and barren mountain,—rising out of the midst of the desert,—that the ten thousand eyes that strained after, sought in vain to pierce the mystery that surrounded them. Perhaps they expected another exhibition of God there similar to the one on Sinai. Its solitary position—its commanding top made it a fit place for such a scene, and as they saw those three forms climb the rugged rocks and precipitous sides, and finally stand on the bold and barren summit, they may have looked for the descent of that wondrous cloud which filled them with such terror on Sinai. God *was* about to speak, but to Moses, and Aaron, and Eleazar alone. The two brothers stood on that high elevation together, and gazed for a moment on the scene below. There were the countless tents of Israel sprinkled over the plain, never more to be entered by Aaron. Farther off arose the city of Edom, and still farther away like a mirror in the landscape, glittered the Dead Sea, whose dark waters slumbered above Sodom and Gomorrah. Behind them rose Mount Seir, and away to the mouth of the Jordan, stretched the valley of El Ghor. All was sad, mournful, and silent. How long the brothers stood and talked together, we cannot tell. Their embraces and repeated farewells were not seen except by Eleazar, and the high priest's prayers were unheard by those who so often had invoked his intercessions at the altar of sacrifice. Aaron's last prayer! the brother and son who heard it, felt that the High Priest had found a Mediator, before whom a broken heart and contrite spirit were the only sacrifice demanded. He had once stayed up Moses' arm in the fight, by his prayers to the God of battle, and now they sustained each other in this last greatest trial. Methinks, that Aaron knelt there, on the top of the barren mountain, and with his hand on the head of his son, commended him to the God of Israel, with tears and intercessions such only as a parent can use. His last instructions had more of heaven than earth in them, and his last farewell was worthy of the High Priest of Israel. Moses, as he stripped him of his sacerdotal robes, doubtless spoke of their speedy meeting in that Canaan, of which the one they sought was but the type. He knew that his own hour was nigh, and that his brother's death was but the prelude to his own. It was a sad task given him to take the sacred vesture from his brother; and, as it were, clothe him while in full health, with his funeral shroud. And the son, the pure-minded, noble, and affectionate son, with what tears and choking grief did he see his father despoiled of his honors, and himself clad in his priestly garments! It was a heavy trial to all—to brother, father, and son, and a mournful scene there on the top of the mountain. But the last embrace was at length given and taken—the last prayer breathed and the High Priest of Israel laid down to die. Glorious was his departure from the top of that lordly mountain—triumphant his last words as his eyes closed on his son, and opened again in heaven.

When the people of Israel saw Moses and Eleazar return alone, and were told that Aaron was dead, they mourned thirty days.

Mount Hor is a lonely peak, seen at a great distance from the desert, and constitutes one of the landmarks by which the Arab guides his way. On its summit is a white building called the tomb of Aaron; Mahometans and Christians reverence it alike, and the sepulchre of the High Priest is safe from the ravages even of he Arab of the desert. A landmark in the bleak scenery, within sight of the desolate city of Edom and its pillared rocks, overlooking the Dead Sea, it is a fit place for the tomb of

Aaron, and stands consecrated forever. An imperishable testimonial of the truth of the Bible—a stern witness of the fulfilment of prophecy—a cursed city and a cursed mountain on either side—it arrests the traveller's eye from afar, and fills him with awe and fear as it silently and perpetually speaks of God.

Turner. Burt.

MOUNT PISGAH.

PERHAPS there is no mountain on our planet, which from its associations has furnished more cheering promises to man than Mount Pisgah. Around its summit cluster some of the most glorious truths of our religion, and a light falls there like the radiance of heaven itself. But of these I do not design to speak. Others have exhibited these truths better than I could; and following out my original plan, I wish merely to describe the scenes connected with this mountain, rather than the truths they develop.

Moses, like Aaron, was denied entrance into the land of Canaan. Though he had braved the wrath of Pharaoh, renounced his worldly expectations, perilled his life, and led on the hosts of Israel for forty years through the wilderness, for the sole purpose of reaching the promised land, his eyes were only to be once gladdened by the sight. He had escaped the wrath of his pursuers—the pestilence that swept so many thousands to death—the bite of the flaming serpents that strewed the camp with so many thousands more—even the decay of the body itself—to die at last by special decree, in sight of the very object of all his toils—the anticipated rest from all his labors. The sea had been passed—the murmurs of the people borne with—the long weary desert travelled over—forty years of the prime of life exhausted, to secure one single object, and then he died with that object unreached, though spread out in all its tempting loveliness before him.

Angry when the people clamored for water—daring to carry out the commands of the Lord in a petulant spirit—assembling the people hastily, without sanctifying them for the great miracle about to be performed, addressing them roughly, and claiming the credit of the miracle, though perhaps unintentionally, saying, "must *we* bring water out of the rock?" and smiting, in his vexation, the rock twice, instead of once, as he had been commanded, and thereby injuring the type,—Moses had so displeased the Lord that he denied him entrance into Canaan.

In whatever relations we behold Moses, with the above single exception, he is ever the same sublime and majestic character. Noble by nature, great by his mission, and greater still by the manner in which he accomplished it, he ever maintains his ascendency over our feelings. We see the fiery promptings of the heart that could not brook oppression, in the bloody vengeance he took on the Egyptian who would trample on his brother. Preferring the desert with freedom to the court of Pharaoh in sight of injustice, he led the life of a fugitive. Called by a voice from heaven to go back to deliver his people, he again trod the courts of the King of Egypt.

But not in the presence of Pharaoh when he withstood the monarch to his face, and brought down the thunders of heaven on his throne—not on the beach of the sea, with one arm upraised towards heaven, and the other stretched out over the water, while the waves that went surging by stopped and crouched at his feet—not in the midst of the raining manna—not in the lifting of the brazen symbol in the midst of the flying serpents, while the moan of suffering and the cries of the dying struggled up from the crowded encampment—not when, between the mountains, his stately form shone in the light of the blazing fiery pillar, while the tread of the mighty multitude shook the earth behind him—nor even when he stood on shaking Sinai, his guard the thunder and his vesture the lightning, and talked with the Eternal as friend talketh with friend,—

not in all these awful relations does he appear to me so majestic and attractive as in this last event of his life.

Behold the white tents of Israel scattered over the plain and swelling knolls at the foot of Mount Nebo. It is a balmy, glorious day The sun is sailing over the encampment, while the blue sky bends like God in love over all things. Here and there a fleecy cloud is hovering over the top of Pisgah, as if conscious of the mysterious scene about to transpire there. The trees stand green and fresh in the sunlight; the lowing of cattle rises through the still atmosphere, and nature is lovely and tranquil, as if no sounds of grief were to disturb her repose.

Amid this beauty and quietness, Moses assembled the children of Israel for the last time, to take his farewell look, and leave his farewell blessing. He cast his eye over the leaders beside him, and over the host, while a thousand contending emotions struggled for the mastery in his bosom. The past with its toils and suffering rose up before him, and how could he part with his children,—murmuring and ungrateful though they had been, whom he had borne on his brave heart for more than forty years? Self-collected and calm he stood before them and gave them his last blessing. He made no complaints—never spoke of his hardships in their behalf; made no allusion to his anguish in leaving them on the very verge of Canaan, the object for which he had toiled so long. He did not even refer to his death. In the magnanimity of his great heart, forgetful of himself, or else not daring to trust his feelings in an allusion to his fate, he closed his sublime address in the following touching language: "The eternal God is thy refuge, and underneath are the everlasting arms; and he shall thrust out the enemy before thee: Israel then shall dwell in safety alone. Happy art thou, O Israel: who is like unto thee, oh people saved by the Lord, the shield of thy help, and who is the sword of thy excellency!" Noble language—noble heart. Carried away in the contemplation of his children's happiness, he burst forth into exclamations of joy in the moment of his deepest distress. But did not that manly voice falter and that stern lip quiver as he advanced to bid them his last adieu? For a moment methinks the rising emotions checked his utterance. They had been the companions of his toil—the objects of his deepest solicitude. A common suffering, a common fate, had bound them to him by a thousand ties. He looked back on the desert: it was past. He looked forward on Canaan: it was near. He turned to the people, and they were weeping. He cast his eye up Nebo, and he knew he must die. Although no complaint escaped his lips—no regret fell from his tongue, a deeper paleness was on his cheek, and a sterner strife in his heart than he had ever felt before. Though outwardly calm, his stern nature shook for a moment like a cedar in a tempest, and then the struggle was over.

His farewell was echoed in melancholy tones from lip to lip through the vast host, as he turned to ascend the mountain. As he advanced from rock to rock, the sobbing of the multitude that followed after, tore his heart-strings like the suffering cry of a child its parent's, and it was long before he dare trust himself to turn and look below. But at length he paused on a high rock and gazed a moment on the scene at his feet. There were the white tents of Jacob glittering in the sun-light, and there the dark mass of Israel's host as they stood and watched the form of their departing leader. Those tents had become familiar to him as household scenes, and as he gazed on them now, far, far beneath him, and saw the cloud overshadowing the mysterious ark, a sigh of unutterable sadness escaped him. He thought of the bones of Joseph he had carried for forty years, that were to rest with his descendants, while he was to be left alone amid the mountains. Again he turned to the ascent, and soon a rock shut him from view, and he passed on alone to the summit.

There God miraculously spread before him all the land of Canaan. He stood a speck on the high crag, and gazed on the lovely scene. Jordan went sweeping by in the glad sunlight. Palm trees shook their green tops in the summer wind, and plains and cities and vineyards spread away in endless beauty before him. But ah, methinks he saw more than the landscape smiling beneath the eastern sky. The history of the future was unrolled before him. He saw the manger of Bethlehem, and also the star that hung over it. There lay glittering in the landscape the sea of Galilee, but he saw more than the water; he beheld the mysterious form walking there in the midst of the midnight storm. He saw Jerusalem in its glory and downfall. He heard the birth-song of the angels, and shout of the shepherds,—and last of all, a mysterious mount rose before him, wrapped in storm and cloud, through whose gloomy foldings gleamed a cross. The clouds rolled away, and lo, the Strength of Israel, the Refuge of Judah, hung in death. Again the vision changed—the sepulchre was open, and like an ascending glory that form rose to heaven.

The scene vanished from his sight, and with the rock for his couch and the blue sky for his covering, he laid down to die. Oh, who can tell what the mighty lawgiver felt, left in that dreadful hour alone! The mystery of mysteries was to be passed. No friend was beside his couch to soothe him, no voice to encourage him in that last, darkest of all human struggles. No one was with him but God, and though with one hand he smote him, with the other he held his dying head. How long was he dying? God alon can answer. What words did his quivering lips last utter? God alone knows. Was his last prayer for Israel?—his last words of the Crucified? From that lonely rock did a shout go up—"Oh Death, where is thy sting? Oh Grave, where is thy victory?" Of that last scene and its changes we know nothing, but when it was over, Moses lay a corpse on the mountain top. And God buried him. There he slept alone—the mountain cloud which night hung round him was his only shroud, and the thunder of the passing storm his only dirge. There he slept while centuries rolled by, his grave unknown and unvisited, until at length he is seen standing on Mount Tabor, with Christ, in the Transfiguration. *Over Jordan at last—in Canaan at last.*

I will not speak here of the instruction this scene affords: but from the very summit of his sorrows, where he had gone to die, Moses for the first time in his life, caught a view of Canaan. He did not know as he went over the rocks, torn and weary, how lovely the prospect was from the top. In this world it frequently happens that when man has reached the place of anguish, God folds away the mist from before his eyes, and the very spot he selected as the receptacle of his tears becomes the place of his highest rapture.

For thirty days did the Israelites mourn at the base of that mountain over their departed leader, and then mournfully struck their tents and moved away. Consecrated by the death of Moses—receiving his last prayer and last sigh, Mount Pisgah stood the *fifth sacred mountain* on the earth.

MOUNT HOREB not being so isolated as Ararat or Sinai, does not occupy so definite a place in nature or history as they. One of the group that surrounds Sinai, it presents the same barren and desolate appearance, and stands amid the same bleak and forbidding scenery. These solemn summits rise together in the same heavens, and the silent language they speak has the same meaning. Still, Horeb has less distinguishing characteristics than Sinai, and the latter overshadows it as much in interest as it does in nature. The Mount of Terror is monarch there in the desert, and all other summits are but his body guard. They witnessed his grand coronation when the law was given, and shook to the thunders that honored the ceremony.

Mount Horeb has not been consecrated once, but thrice, and hence has a threefold claim for a place amid the immortal list of Sacred Mountains. Moses learned his first lessons around its base, and amid its solitudes formed the thoughtful, stern, and decided character which rendered him fit to be the leader of Israel. When in his impetuous youth he slew the Egyptian that would trample on his countryman, he came thither to escape the penalty of the deed. After the first gust of indignation had swept by, and he saw the lifeless corpse at his feet, alarm took the place of passion, and hastily covering the dead man in the sand, he fled to the desert. Month after month he wandered about Horeb, thinking of Egypt and the royal court he dared not enter. Away from the temptations of the palace, and beyond the reach of the conflicting motives that might sway him there, he trod the desert a free man. With nought but Nature and God to teach him, his character must be simple and manly, and his principles upright and pure. Amid the grand and striking features of mountain scenery, he could not but learn to hate tyranny and love freedom still more, and when, at length, his character was settled on a broad and permanent basis, God sent him back to Egypt to deliver his people.

Wandering one morning along the slopes of Horeb, he saw before him a solitary bush blazing from top to bottom, but still unconsumed. Every branch was a fiery branch and every leaf a leaf of fire that glowed unwasted in the still flame. As he stood amazed and awe-struck at the sight, a voice whose tones were yet to be familiar to his ear exclaimed, "Take thy shoes from off thy feet, for the place on which thou standest is Holy Ground." Here Moses received his first commission, and here was God's first outward demonstration to him in behalf of his people.

In the exciting scenes through which he afterwards passed in Egypt, he may have entirely forgotten Horeb. But after the plagues, and death, and flight, and pursuit, and Red Sea passage, and overthrow of his enemies, had all been left behind, and the host of Israel entered the desert, the familiar scenery he began to approach must have waked up strange associations in his heart. At length the well-remembered form of Horeb, where he had wandered lonely and solitary, self-exiled from his home, rose before him. A gloomy fugitive he first saw that desolate mountain in the distance;—a leader of a mighty people, and the chosen of God, he pitched his tent the second time at its base. Doubtless his first inverview with the Deity here, caused him to expect some other revelations now that the commission he had given him had been fulfilled. How much his early experience had to do with his encamping on this spot with the host of Israel it is impossible to tell; but that he should expect that God who had first sent him forth should here give him further instructions was most natural. His expectations were not disappointed, and Sinai and Horeb together became the scene of the most wondrous events of human history. The shadow of Sinai falls over Horeb, and they stand together in immortal brotherhood. They cannot well be separated in contemplating the revelations of God to his people, on their journey from Egypt to Canaan, and hence I have not attempted it.

Still, there are other scenes connected with Horeb, in which Sinai is not mentioned. Twice had it been honored by the presence of Deity, which had so consecrated it that we find the angel of the Lord afterwards calling it "*the Mount of God.*" It was however destined for a third baptism. When Elijah, hunted by Jezebel, fled for his life, he wandered across the desert to this mountain. His prayers had brought rain upon the parched and desolate earth, but his sword had also drank the blood of the prophets of Baal, and Jezebel had sent him word that she would do to him as he had done to her prophets; and so he fled into the wilderness and sat down under a juniper tree and prayed for death. Weary and discouraged, the hunted fugitive laid down and slept on the barren heath, when the angel of the Lord touched him and bade him arise and go to Mount Horeb. Elijah started for the desert, and after travelling for more than a month, he at length, worn and exhausted, came to the mountain, and took up his solitary lodgings in a cave. How many desolate days and lonely nights he passed there we know not, but broken in spirit, nay, his faith itself weak and well nigh gone, his hours whether few or many were full of despondency and sorrow. Both the blessings and judgments he had brought on Israel, attended, though they had been, with mira cles, had failed to turn the people from their wickedness. That Elijah was still in the despairing mood which caused him to pray under the juniper tree for death is evident both from the interrogation of the Deity and the reply of the prophet. "The Lord said unto him, What doest thou here, Elijah? And he said, I have been very jealous for the Lord God of Hosts, for the children of Israel have forsaken thy covenants, thrown down thy altars, and slain thy prophets with the sword; and I, even I only am left, and they seek my life. And he said, Go forth and stand upon the mount." Jehovah was about to reveal himself, and Elijah evidently expected some exhibition of divine goodness or power, though he was not prepared for the scene which was about to transpire. Before he reached the entrance of his cave he heard a roar louder than the sea, that arrested his footsteps and sent the blood back to his heart. The next moment there came a blast of wind, as if the last chain that bound it had suddenly been thrown off and it had burst forth in all its unrestrained and limitless energy. In the twinkling of an eye the sun was blotted out by the cloud of dust, and the fragments that filled the air as it whirled them in fierce eddies onward. It shrieked and howled around the mouth of the cave, while the fierce hissing sound of its steady pressure against the heart of the mountain was more terrible than its ocean-like roar. Before its fury and strength rocks were loosened from their beds and hurled through the gloom—the earth rent where it passed, and so boundless seemed its strength that the steady mountain threatened to lift from its base and be carried away. Amid this deafening uproar and confusion and darkness and terror, the stunned and awe-struck Elijah expected to see the form of Jehovah moving; but that resistless blast, strewing the sides of Horeb with wreck and chaos was not God in motion:

> "'Twas but the whirlwind of his *breath*,
> Announcing danger, wreck, and death."

The hurricane passed by, and that wild strife of the elements ceased; but before the darkened heavens could clear themselves the prophet heard a rumbling sound in the bowels of the mountain, and the next moment an earthquake was on the march. Stern Horeb rocked to and fro like a vessel in a storm, and its bosom parted with the sound of thunder before the convulsive throbs that seemed rending the very heart of nature. Fathomless abysses opened on every side, and huge precipices, toppling over the chasms at their base, went thundering through the darkness. The fallen prophet lay on the floor of his cavern and listened to the grinding, crushing sound around and beneath him, and the steady shocks more terrible than all that ever and anon shook the heights, thinking that Jehovah at last stood before him. Surely it was his mighty hand that laid on that trembling, tottering mountain, and his strong arm that rocked it so wildly on its base. No, "God was not in the earthquake."

> "'Twas but the thundering of his car,
> The trampling of his steeds from far."

The commotion ceased, and Nature stood "and calmed her ruffled frame:" but in the deep, ominous silence that followed, there seemed a foreshadowing of some new terror, and lo, the heavens were suddenly on fire, and a sheet of flame fell like falling lightning from the sky. Its lurid light pierced to the depths of Elijah's cavern till it glowed like an oven, and from base to summit of Mount Horeb there went up a vast cloud of smoke, fast and furious, while the entire sides flowed with torrents of fire. The mountain glowed with a red heat, and stood like a huge burning furnace under a burning heaven, and groaned on its ancient seat as if in torture. But God was not in the fiery storm.

> "'Twas but the lightning of his eye"

that had kindled that mountain into a blaze, and filled the air with flame.

But this too passed by, and what new scene of terror could rise worthy to herald the footsteps of God—what greater outward grandeur could surround his presence? The astonished prophet still lay upon his face wrapped in wonder, and filled with fear at these exhibitions of Almighty power, waiting for the next scene in this great drama, when suddenly through the deep quiet, and breathless hush that had succeeded the earthquake and the storm, there arose "a still small voice," the like of which had never met his ear before. It was "small and still," but it thrilled the prophet's frame with electric power, and rose so sweet and clear,

> "That all in heaven and earth might hear;
> It spoke of peace—it spoke of love,
> It spoke as angels speak above."

And God was in the voice. The prophet knew that He was nigh, and, rising up, wrapped his mantle about his face, and went to the mouth of the cave, and reverently stood and listened. Oh, who can tell the depth and sweetness of the tones of that voice which the Lord of love deemed worthy to announce his coming. A ransomed spirit's harp—an angel's lute—a seraph's song, could not have moved the prophet so. But while his whole being, soul and body, trembled to its music, a sterner voice met his ear, saying, "What doest thou here, Elijah?" The prophet again poured the tale of his woes and of Israel's sin into the Infinite bosom. His wrongs were promised redress, and Israel deliverance; and the hunted exile went boldly back to his people, and Horeb again stood silent and alone in the desert.

Bartlett. Burt.

MOUNT CARMEL.

VII

MOUNT CARMEL

MOUNT CARMEL stands by the sea, lifting its head two thousand feet above the water, looking off on Sharon towards the south, while inland Tabor shows dim through the hazy atmosphere. Its shape is that of a flattened cone, and it is one of the most picturesque objects in that land of glorious associations. Two scenes, totally different, yet thrilling in the extreme, have transpired on its summit. Elijah and Mount Carmel go together, and no time nor change can separate them in human history.

Under the reign of the despot Ahab, Israel had forsaken the commandments of God and his worship, and gone over to idolatry till vice and cruelty covered the land. To bring the nation to reflection God declared through Elijah that no rain should fall on the earth for years; and lo, the heavens were shut up and became like brass over the thirsty fields. Every thing withered up —the corr shrivelled and died—the grass shrunk away and turned red in the fierce heat—the very trees drooped and died, and the once fat herds, reduced to skeletons, swarmed over the fields in search of food and water. The harvest remained ungathered, and the farmer looked with anxious, and then despairing heart on his barren fields and empty granaries. Men husbanded the little grain that was left, and all over Israel, food was measured out by piecemeal, for want began to stare them in face. The first year men were impoverished, the second ruined in their fortunes, but the third brought famine and all its horrors. Children pleading for bread died in their parents' arms—the old yielded up the ghost with a groan, and the strong-limbed, fell bloated, on their own thresholds, and woe, and wretchedness, were on every side. At first, Ahab was angry with Elijah, who had predicted this calamity, and attempted to slay him as the cause of it; but the prophet fled from his hand. But, at length, the haughty king was frightened into apparent meekness, and then the prophet presented himself before him. The hunted fugitive trod the courts of the palace without fear, and more like a king than their owner, and stood with a stern and haughty brow before the royal despot. The king looked on him a moment in surprise, as he stood wrapped in his mantle before him, then said, "Art thou he that troubleth Israel?" The roused prophet, whose heart had bled over the sufferings of his beloved country, who would gladly have sacrificed his life to have saved it, could not brook the charge implied in this question. Hurling back the accusation in the very teeth of the king, he said, "*I have not trou bled Israel, but thou and thy father's house, in that ye have forsaken the commandments of the Lord and thou hast followed Baalim.*" "*Thou*, proud monarch, art the enemy of thy country; *thou* hast brought down the curse of heaven; on *thy* head rests the guilt of all this woe and death." Such was the language the despised, and poor, and exiled prophet uttered in the ears of the astonished Ahab. Conscience had at length awoke, and he dared not resent it, but allowed himself to be bearded on his very throne, surrounded by his vassals. Elijah saw that he was partially humbled by fear—and well he might be at the spectacle his country presented--and so immediately proposed a trial of the respective claims of the prophets of the Lord and those of Baal: "Gather me," said he, "all Israel unto Mount Carmel, and with them four hundred and fifty of the prophets of Baal, and four hundred more of the prophets of the groves who sit at Jezebel's table." A strange proposal for a public criminal to make to a king, but there was something about him that awed the monarch, so that he dared not refuse his consent. That plain-clad man in his mantle, who had been a by-word for children for years, now dictated to the king, who had hunted him like a common felon, the length and breadth of Israel. His order was obeyed, and lo, all Israel came flocking to Carmel. Every road was thronged with the eager thousands: on foot, in carriages, and on horseback they went streaming onward, till every highway leading to the mountain was filled with the dust of hasty travellers. In the barren fields through which they rode—in the wan and haggard faces that stared on them as they passed, they saw evidence enough that Israel was troubled, and that it was time the cause was made known.

The prophets of Baal, and of the groves, eight hundred and fifty of them in all, went in the pomp becoming their high station and power, and thus priest and people thronged together to this strange rendezvous. Without a friend to cheer him, unless perchance Obadiah was with him,—on foot and alone, Elijah trod his weary way to the same solemn gathering. Behold the top of Carmel covered with the multitude! Below them heaves the blue Mediterranean, whose restless waters lose themselves in the distance; behind them is Palestine in its beauty, and, far away, the snow-capt heights of Lebanon fringe the horizon. It is a glorious spectacle beneath and around, and the solemn murmur of the sea perchance rises over the hum of the multitude. But soon one form and one voice arrest every eye and ear. Wrapped in his mantle, Elijah stands on the lordly summit, and casting his eye over the landscape, and over the throng, at length breaks forth: "*How long halt ye between two opinions? If the Lord be God, follow him; but if Baal then follow him.*" He paused, and gazed sternly on the thousands about him, but not a voice broke the ominous silence. There was an air of authority about him that awed even the prophets of Baal; and, in the confidence of a king rather than with the humility of a proscribed man, he made a proposal which should forever settle who was the true God, and which were the false. "I," said Elijah, "am the only prophet of the Lord left, while here are four hundred and fifty prophets of Baal. But let them now take two bullocks, and cut one in pieces, and lay it on wood without fire; and I will dress the other bullock and lay it on wood, and put no fire under; and they shall call on their God, and I will call on the Lord, and the God that answereth by fire let him be God." "It is well spoken," murmured the multitude; "let it be tried." Whether the prophets wished to come to this conclusive issue or not, they were forced to it by the people. Doubtless, they feared a failure, but they hoped their numbers and their power might overawe Elijah, and it might be a mutual failure, and then the prophet's doom was sealed. He had called all Israel together, and the people were on the stretch of expectation, and any thing short of overwhelming success would be disgrace and death. "*And I am left alone*." Yes, thou *art* alone, Elijah, and around thee are nearly a thousand vindictive foes, thirsting for thy blood; and if thy God answers not by fire then wilt thou thyself be offered up here on the mountain, a sacrifice to human hate. True, thou standest proudly there, with thy uplifted arm pointing towards heaven, and thy prophet's mantle wrapped about thee, and thy voice is like one who knows the secrets of God; but woe to thee if thou hast deceived thyself and this mighty assembly.

Thus thought many a heart as they saw Elijah, by one single act, bring the reputation of God and his own life into apparent jeopardy. But now there was no retreat to either party, and the prophets of Baal cut their bullock in pieces, and laid it on the wood, under the open sky, and began to pray. There was no room for deception here—all was open and clear, and every eye could see the fire that should fall from the cloudless heavens above. All was silent expectation and breathless anxiety as this strange scene commenced. The sun had just risen over the Holy Land, flooding Mount Carmel with his beams, as those four hundred and fifty prophets knelt, in one dense mass, around the altar and began their supplications. At first, solemn and fervent, as became the dignity of the occasion, they besought Baal, for his honor and for the sake of his followers, to hear them. To send down fire, and thus forever to silence the tongue of this hostile prophet, was a small matter for one so powerful. But no fire descended,—the sun rode quietly up the heavens,—the deep heaved calmly below, and the morning wind went seaward as gaily as ever. Thus they prayed till noon, while the people looked on. But at length frenzy took the place of supplication, and it was one wild shout around that bullock, as it lay smoking in the mid-day sun. Elijah till now had stood apart and quietly surveyed the scene, but as the excited throng began their mad outcries and frantic gestures, crying, "O Baal hear us!" his long suppressed scorn broke forth, and he taunted them in the midst of their ravings, and said, "Cry aloud, for he is a god; perhaps he is busy talking, and cannot attend to you immediately; or he is pursuing his foe, and cannot stop; or perhaps he is on a journey, or asleep. Shout louder, and wake up your God." Bitter words, that only increased the frenzy of those to whom they were addressed, and they leaped upon the altar, flinging their arms aloft, crying out still more frantically, "O Baal, hear us!" They cut themselves with knives and lancets, till the blood streamed over the bullock, and shouted till Mount Carmel rung with their turbulent cries, and became a scene of indescribable confusion; but still the heavens were silent and serene as ever; no voice answered them—no fire came down.

At length the people began to tire of this exciting but useless scene, and the prophets themselves gave up in despair. Then came Elijah's turn. The sun was stooping towards the sea, and the time of the evening sacrifice approached. Standing up, he called the people to him, and, as they clustered around, he repaired the long neglected altar of the Lord, and placed upon it twelve stones for the twelve tribes of Israel. He then dug a trench around it, and having placed the wood on the altar, and the bullock on the wood, told the spectators to pour four barrels of water over them. They did so. "Do it the second time," said he, and they did it the second time, and the third time, till the trench was full to the brim, and the wood and the sacrifice were flooded. Here could be no deception, no concealed fire, nothing which could allow the prophets of Baal to declare the whole a trick, for the altar was flowing with water.

All is now ready; the disappointed prophets and Israel's thousands are looking anxiously on. The blazing fireball is hanging over the waves below, and already the sea breeze is stealing landward, for the time of the evening sacrifice has arrived. Elijah advances towards the altar, with uncovered head and solemn countenance, but with no hesitation or alarm in his glance. His step is firm and his eye serene, as he moves across the space between him and the spectators. Yet, methinks, I hear a voice saying, "Gird now thyself, Elijah, for thine hour has come. Thy God and the God of Abraham, and Isaac, and Jacob, thou hast cast on one bold issue. Woe for thee, and woe for Israel, if thou failest!"

But he shall not fail. He kneels and prays. There is no confession of sin, no pleading for pardon, for he is not asking for blessings on his own head, or on that of his country: he is asking God to vindicate himself, and make good his given word. There seems no necessity for strong crying and earnest supplication; yet in that sudden outburst of "*Hear me, O Lord, hear me!*" I see the mighty wrestling of a mighty soul. He prays fervently, but solemnly. There is no contortion, no assumed tone or manner, as with uplifted hands he exclaims, "LORD GOD OF ABRAHAM, ISAAC, AND OF ISRAEL, LET IT BE KNOWN THIS DAY THAT THOU ART GOD IN ISRAEL, AND THAT I AM THY SERVANT, AND THAT I HAVE DONE ALL THESE THINGS AT THY WORD. HEAR ME, OH LORD, HEAR ME, THAT THIS PEOPLE MAY KNOW THAT THOU ART THE LORD GOD, AND THAT THOU HAST TURNED THEIR HEART BACK AGAIN." He ceased, and lo! from the cloudless heavens fire fell like falling lightning, and the bullock smoked amid the water that flooded it, and a swift vapor rose from the top of Carmel, and all was over! There lay the ashes of the sacrifice, and there the dry trenches, and there, too, knelt the awe-struck prophet. For a moment the silence of the grave hung over that solitary mountain, as the astonished multitude hid their faces in the earth, but the next moment there arose a murmur, swelling gradually louder and louder like the gathering roar of the sea, till, drowning every other sound, it rolled gloriously towards heaven—"*The Lord he is the God; Jehovah he is the God!*" 'Twas done; Truth had triumphed, and Israel was saved.

But Elijah had not yet fulfilled his mission. Turning sternly to the people, he bade them seize the prophets of Baal, and not let one of them escape. Prayers and entreaties were alike in vain. Though they crowd around the just now despised exile with tears, he has no pity for their fate. God and his country demand their death, and down the mountain slope they are dragged by the indignant people, and there, by the margin of the brook Kishon, Elijah slays them, and the parched earth drinks up their blood.

Still the prophet's work is not done; his country's enemies are destroyed, but her sufferings are not allayed. The crowd may return home, but he, accompanied by his servant, reascends Carmel. Standing on the now silent and solitary summit, in sight of the forsaken altars, he surveys for a moment the heavens above him, and the scene around him; the sun is just bathing his burning forehead in the western wave ere he sinks to rest, and not a cloud is on the brazen sky. Casting himself upon the earth, and burying his face between his knees, again he prays. But where is the lofty bearing and stern aspect that just now awed the people, as he brought fire from heaven? Gone with the fulfilment of his task. He was then defending the God of Israel before scoffers and idolaters, and his voice and aspect became his great mission. But now he is pleading for pardon for his suffering, sinful country; he is entreating God to take his erring people once more to his arms, and pour upon them his blessings, and he is in the dust, as it becomes such a mediator. For three years and a half not a drop of rain has fallen in Israel, and he now beseeches the Lord to water the earth and stay the famine and woe of the land.

As he closed his prayer, he bade his servant go and look towards the sea. He obeyed, and returned, saying, "I see nothing." Again the prophet poured his supplications into the bosom of the God of Jacob, and again sent his servant to see if there were signs of rain. Again he returned as before. Still Elijah's faith did not falter. Again he prayed, and again sent his servant, till the seventh time. But the seventh time he came back, saying, "There is a little cloud rising out of the sea, like a man's hand." It was enough—Faith was satisfied, and Elijah arose and said to his servant, "Go up, say unto Ahab, Prepare thy chariot, and get thee down that the rain stop thee not." He heard the sound of the coming storm before it arrived, aye, heard it long before, in the silence that followed the death of the prophets. And, lo! what a sight appeared from Mount Carmel. Dark and angry clouds began to roll up the scorching heavens,—the sun went down in gloom,—the sea rose and shook itself to meet the coming tempest,—fierce lightnings traversed the angry masses, as they pushed themselves upward,—the thunder came muttering over the Mediterranean, as it rolled its vexed waters against the base of the mountain,—the sound of wind and rain was borne landward, and day was turned into sudden night, as the storm burst on the land of Israel. The thirsty and barren earth again smiled in verdure, and the long curse was removed. What a day of terror and of grace that had been to Israel, and as the prophet lay that night and listened to the descending rain, methinks his heart swelled with deeper gratitude than ever before to the God of his fathers.

Mount Carmel still stands by the sea, and

overlooks the same prospect, but the people of God are no longer there. Priest and prophet have disappeared, and there is no Elijah now to plead in their behalf. A Turkish mosque stands where arose the altar of God, and the Muezzin's voice rings where arose the prayer of the prophet.

Harding. Burt.

MOUNT LEBANON.

VIII

MOUNT LEBANON

LEBANON is not an isolated peak, but a chain of mountains running through the south of Syria. There are two grand ridges rising above the rest, called Libanus or Lebanon, and Antelibanus. The name signifies white mountain, and was given to this range from the white appearance its snow-capt summits present, and also perhaps from the limestone rocks that form it. The highest mountain in Syria, covered with snow both in summer and winter, Lebanon naturally became a marked object to the Israelites in that warm climate. Still it has been consecrated by no great event—no manifestation of God there has made its soil sacred to the pilgrim, and it has not that claim to a place among the list of immortal mountains that others possess. It is, nevertheless, mentioned so frequently in the Bible, and spoken of with such delight by prophets and kings, and, indeed, used so often by God himself to illustrate his declarations to his people, that we have come to regard it as a holy mountain. Besides, the wood for Solomon's temple was cut from its slopes, and many of the sacred utensils were made from its fragrant cedars. Christ and the church are also likened to Lebanon, from their fruitfulness, and fragrance, and glory. Even Jerusalem was sometimes called Lebanon, because the temple and the houses were built almost entirely of its cedars.

The Lebanon range furnished several peaks more or less elevated, and though the highest was usually white with snow, those more depressed were covered with vineyards, while fountains leaped from the declivities and cool brooks wound through the fragrant fields that carpeted their sides—now glowing in the sunlight as they crept over the landscape, and now lost amid the green shrubbery that clustered on the shores, until they at length reached the plain and flowed away towards the streams of Abana, and Parphar, and Jordan. As the traveller approached Lebanon, the cool breeze that fell from its summit made him forget the heat and toil of the way, and bless the heights that poured such freshness and health into his path. And as he lifted his eyes, the scene before him ravished his senses. All along the hill-sides, and over the rolling heights, spread away vineyards in every direction, while here and there, half hid amid the grapes, peeped forth the vine-dresser's cottage, and clustering trees, and babbling streams, and all the beauty and verdure of an eastern clime seemed to have been gathered there in their greatest richness and variety, while to finish the picture, endless forests of cedars waved along the top—a green crown to all the beauty below, making it indeed "the glory of Lebanon." Those lofty cedars caught the first sunlight in the land of Israel, and on their green tops the last beams of day lingered long after deep shadow filled the plains below. The fruitful fields and pure water, and spring-like verdure and coolness, made the mountain known even beyond the boundaries of Canaan. Moses had heard of it and longed to see it before he died. "I pray thee," said he, as he besought the Lord to let him enter Canaan, "let me go over and see the good land that is beyond Jordan, and *that goodly mountain, Lebanon.*"

One who has never travelled in a warm climate and a desert country, cannot appreciate the feelings of the inhabitants towards a forest-covered and fruitful mountain. By the coolness it imparts to the atmosphere, the pure water it sends to the vales, and the wood it furnishes to the builder, it is viewed one of the greatest blessings of the land.

Such was Lebanon when Jerusalem was in its glory. David sang of it—to have "his fruit shake like Lebanon" was to make one rich in blessings. To "grow like a cedar in Lebanon" was to flourish in unchecked vigor. Solomon, too, in less exalted strains, sung of the "wood of Lebanon," of its fragrance and its streams. The countenance of "his beloved was like Lebanon," and "excellent as the cedars." Isaiah thought of it in his moments of highest rapture, and as he foresaw the increase of the church of God, he bursts forth, "the glory of Lebanon shall come unto thee, the fir-tree, and the pine-tree, and the box together, to beautify the place of my sanctuary, and I will make the place of my feet glorious." Jeremiah makes God compare the royal house of Judah to Lebanon, saying, "thou art Gilead unto me, and the head of Lebanon." Hosea in predicting the future greatness of Israel exclaims, "thus saith the Lord, I will be as dew unto Israel; he shall grow as the lily and cast forth his roots as Lebanon. His branches shall spread, and his beauty shall be as the olive tree, and his smell as Lebanon. They that dwell under his shadow shall return, they shall revive as the corn and grow as the vine, the scent thereof shall be as the wine of Lebanon." Thus did the poet and the prophet make use of Lebanon to illustrate the truths of heaven, consecrating its name, if not itself, the world over.

The forests of cedars that covered its heights must have been well nigh exhaustless, for not only was the temple built from them, and most of Jerusalem itself, but it furnished all the timber for shipping to the Tyrians and Sidonians, then the greatest commercial nations on the globe. Here too, the Assyrians and Chaldeans, when they overran Syria, Canaan, and Phenicia, obtained their wood to carry on their sieges; and yet to expiate sin, " Lebanon is not sufficient to burn, nor the beasts thereof sufficient for a burnt-offering."

but the glory of Lebanon is gone—the cedars that covered it are fallen, and the nation that crowded at its base is peeled and scattered over the earth. The curse of the Holy One has fallen upon it, and the prophecy that "Lebanon should fall" and her "tall cedars be cut down," has been fulfilled. Of all her ancient groves, but few now remain, and they are bereft of their former glory. Mere monuments of the past, just sufficient by contrast to make the desolation complete, they arrest the eye of the traveller only to move his heart with sorrow.

Villages are still scattered over the heights, and the vine-dresser's voice is still heard as of old, but all else how changed! Innumerable convents dot the sides of the ancient pride of Israel, and the Maronite is the chief dweller there. The terraced vineyards are beautiful along the slopes, and the great "cedar grove" belting the highest summit of the mountain, together with the ruins of ancient temples slowly crumbling back to dust, are worthy of the pilgrim's toil. But, alas, the ancient shrine is shattered, and Mahometan rites have taken the place of the Hebrew's prayer and sacrifice.

From the sea, Lebanon is still glorious to behold. Rising ten thousand feet in the heavens, it rolls its white and ancient peaks along the sky, as if it constituted the outer wall of the earth. Running from the north-east to the south-west, it stretches from opposite Damascus to the plains of Esdraelon, into which it seems to sink. The great land-mark of that country, it stands unwasted by the ravages of time, a silent witness of the truth of revelation, and the fulfilment of prophecy. Nations may be born and die, at its base cities sink and rise, and the records of human history fail; yet so long as the Bible remains, Lebanon shall stand as one of its witnesses—a perpetual memento of departed glory. Around its hallowed form rests an atmosphere of beauty, and to the end of time the traveller, pausing at its base, shall sigh as he remembers how the poets of Israel struck their lyres, and the prophets of God breathed forth their numbers in its praise.

IX

MOUNT ZION

PERHAPS there is no name in human history the mention of which awakens so many thrilling associations as that of Zion. It not only represents the ancient Jewish church, and all that was dear and holy in her, but it is applied to the Christian church at the present day. Confined to no sect and no clime, and no language; it embraces in its catholicity all who love God, binding them in one endearing epithet together to the end of time. 'ZION!" there is something sad as well as delightful in the word, and the heart pauses over it with a sigh half of regret and half of affection, for the past, while its mournful history, rises to view. Zion has had tears as

Balmar. Burt.

MOUNT ZION.

well as raptures, suffering as well as joy, and her note of lamentation has arisen as often as her song of thanksgiving. He who has kept a record of her tears knows full well her conflicts and her trials, and that from the time of her toilsome flight through the wilderness and desert to the land of Canaan till now, she has been a stranger and sojourner in a world of wicked men. Now scattered to the four winds of heaven, her children sad captives and her home the prey of the spoiler, she has wept unavailing tears at the feet of her spoilers; and now rent by inward dissensions and secret foes, she has committed suicide around her own altars. But still her very dust has been precious in the eyes of him who hath formed her for himself; and out of the most hopeless bondage, from deepest ruin, he has again called her, and adorned her with robes of beauty, and put a crown of glory on her head, and made her enemies to flee before her. Amid the amazement of those who believed her ruin complete, and the astonishment of her friends, a voice has been heard to say,

> "Zion still is well beloved."

The literal Mount Zion was one of the hills on which Jerusalem was built. It stood near Mount Moriah, where Abraham offered up Isaac to the Lord, and witnessed that greatest triumph of human faith; and centuries afterwards, when the temple covered the summit of the former, it formed the heart and strength of the city. Situated at the southern extremity, it rose above every other part of Jerusalem, and came in time to stand for the city itself. At first it seems strange that Zion should have become a word filled with such endearing associations to the Jews. They could never let it go from them when speaking of their city. If her strength as a fortress was spoken of, the language was, "Walk about *Zion*, and go round about her; tell the towers thereof: mark ye well her bulwarks, and consider her palaces;"—

if her elevation, it was, "The holy hill of *Zion.*" God's affection for his people was expressed by his love for *Zion*, "He loveth the gates of Zion," "The Lord hath chosen Zion." As if this were not enough, they and their city together are called "Daughter of Zion." Occupied by the son of Jesse, it became the "City of David," the representative of all that was dear and cherished in Israel. Hence it was called also the "Holy hill of Zion, whither the tribes went up, the tribes of the Lord unto the testimony of Israel." It was "God's hill, in which it delighted him to dwell." Thus every thing conspired to render "Zion" the spell-word of the nation, and on its summit the heart of Israel seemed to lie and throb. While it remained unshaken by its foes, hope and joy reigned in every bosom, but when the feet of the spoiler trod its sacred top, and his conquering troops swept over it, a cry of despair went up around its towers.

How often the name is on the lips of David; and every string of his harp seems tuned to utter "*Zion.*" In a burst of lofty enthusiasm, carried away by a sudden transport as he contemplates its glory and strength, he exclaims, "*Beautiful for situation, the joy of the whole earth is Mount Zion; God is known in her palaces for a refuge. Let Mount Zion rejoice, let the daughters of Judah be glad, for this God is our God for ever and ever.*"

But perhaps there is no exhibition of the love the Hebrews bore for it so touching as the reply they made when captives in Babylon, to those who required of them a song. "The joy of the earth" had been ravaged, and that "holy hill," so "beautiful for situation" laid desolate by the enemy. Its palaces were broken down, and a heap of ruins alone marked the spot where the "City of David" arose. On its top Israel's thousands had stood and battled for its safety. Their fearful war-cry had rung along its streets, as the banner of David rose and fell in the doubtful fight, till borne back and overwhelmed, leaving thousands of corpses as bloody testimonials of the desperate conflict, they at length yielded to numbers and Jerusalem fell. A multitude of captives graced the triumphal entrance of the victors into Babylon, and the city shook to the shouts of welcome. But the pageantry was soon forgotten, and the prisoners became objects only of idle curiosity as they moved sadly along the streets, or sat in groups under the trees of the public walks. Methinks I see that little band, as strolling one day through the city they sat down by its fountains and listened to the murmur of the streams that swept by. The scene was beautiful, and it reminded them of the hill of Zion where they had so often strayed—the home of their hearts—never to be seen again. As they thus sat and conversed in their native tongue, filled with sad remembrances,—their neglected harps hanging on the willows—the heartless and curious passed by, and stopped to view their strange apparel and listen to their still stranger language. As they saw their harps hanging beside them they asked for a native song. The hearts of the captives were sad enough before, but this sudden recalling of the joys of the past was too much for their overburdened feelings, and a burst of tears was the only answer, as they shook their heads in mournful silence.

That day of bitterness they could never forget, and whenever memory recalled it the heart seemed to live over again its hour of woe, and they said, " By the rivers of Babylon there we sat down, yea, we wept when we remembered Zion. We hung our harps upon the willows in the midst thereof. For there they that carried us away captive required of us a song, and they that wasted us asked for mirth, saying, Sing us one of the songs of Zion. How shall we sing the Lord's song in a strange land. If I forget thee, Oh Jerusalem, let my right hand forget her cunning. If I do not remember thee, let my tongue cleave to the roof of my mouth if I prefer not Jerusalem above my chief joy." They did not forget her, and the city of David once more rose over the hill of Zion, and the banner of Israel again floated from its heights, for God had remembered her tears and forgiven her sins.

Years passed, and though visited by misfortune and ruin for its departures from the Lord, Zion still arose in its glory and strength. But at length its long line of kings disappeared—the Roman occupied it, and the eagles of Cæsar took the place of the banner of David. Still Mount Zion stood, beautiful as of old, the pride of the conqueror; but its cup of iniquity was fast filling to the brim. Shiloh had come, and the rejected Saviour, as he overlooked the city, wept in view of its approaching doom. There was Mount Moriah lifting the temple on high, whose glorious form dazzled the eyes of the beholder as the sunbeams fell upon it; and there, higher yet, Mount Zion, with its countless palaces and domes and towers of strength, before him. His heart yearned over the "glory of the earth," and the daughter of Zion looked beautiful upon her throne of hills; and as he thought of the past—of her toils and sufferings—of her former faithfulness, and all that God had done for her, words of deepest love were heard to fall from his lips. But amid them was also heard the startling language, "*Behold your house is left unto you desolate.*"

The last drop in the cup of crime, the crowning guilt at length came,—Zion crucified her Saviour. Then the long delayed curse fell, and Roman legions girdled the city. Mount Zion became the scene of the severest strife that had ever wasted it, and of the keenest sufferings its crimes had ever brought upon it. Although a troop of flaming seraphs had stooped on the temple, and with the words "let us depart," wheeled away to heaven again, and chariots of fire had been seen jostling against each other in the evening heavens, and a flaming sword been suspended over the city, and the woe of the denouncing prophet heard along its walls, still the doomed inhabitants believed them not as omens of evil. Under their ancient banner they once more rallied for the conflict, and for a long time Mount Zion stood like a tower of strength amid her foes. Beating back the tide of battle from her sides, she proved worthy of her olden renown. Standing shoulder to shoulder on that glorious hill-top, the tens of thousands of Israel's warriors presented an unbroken front to the foe, and their shout went up as strong and terrible as when Joshua led them on to victory. "*Zion shall be ploughed as a field, and Jerusalem shall become heaps!*" Impossible! "Walk about Zion and go round about her," "mark her bulwarks, tell the towers thereof, consider her palaces," number if ye can her warriors, proud of their strength and confident in their resources. But the decree has gone forth, "*Zion shall be ploughed as a field.*" Famine is stronger than the arm of the warrior, and inward dissensions more wasting than the sword of the enemy. The banner of Israel still floats in the breeze, but it waves over the blood of her children. Pestilence has entered the gates, and the groans of the dying rise from every house. Bloated forms are seen staggering round the empty market places, chewing wisps of straw and leather for food, and falling dead in their footsteps. Despairing eyes, and wan and haggard faces stare from every window, and corpses are hurried in crowds over the walls, till even the enemy turn away from the fetid air. The strong fall on the weak and tear them asunder, to get the morsel they have swallowed, and mothers devour even their own offspring. The thunder of engines is heard against the walls without, and the clash of steel mingles in the wild confusion. Yet even amid this terror and woe, Zion fights against herself and strives to swell the slaughter of her own children. At length the last day and last hour come — the temple is on fire and blazes balefully up from Mount Moriah—the eagles of Cæsar flash along the crowded streets, and the shrieks of the flying and the shout of the struggling, mingling with the crackling of the flames, rise over the city. Zion at length yields, the last strong-hold is taken, and the spoiler roams unchecked through the streets. "Jerusalem is in heaps," destruction has done her worst, and silence reigns amid the desolation.

Their task at length accomplished, the victors take up their line of march, followed by the long train of captives, and depart. As they ascend the last slope that overlooks Jerusalem, that mournful band pause and turn to give a farewell look to Mount Zion. As they behold it strewed with burning ruins and think of their desolate homes never to be rebuilt or revisited, and see but a cloud of smoke where the glorious temple stood, tears of unavailing sorrow stream from their eyes, and a "note of lamentation swells upon the breeze."

Years have passed by, and the plough-share is driven over the top of Zion. Where its towers and palaces stood grain waves in the passing wind, or ruins overlaying each other attest the truth of the Word of God. The Arab spurs his steed along the forsaken streets, or scornfully stands on Mount Zion and surveys the forsaken city of God.

But the promise is still sure—Zion is not forgotten, nor is her glory gone. The church of God still lives and flourishes in more than her ancient beauty. Kingdoms may rise and fall like waves along the sea, and the strongest monuments of human skill crumble to dust, and the earth itself change places, Zion is still secure. No foe can finally prevail against her, nor even time, under whose corroding tooth all things disappear, touch her life. She has brighter palaces than those which adorned Jerusalem, and firmer towers and bulwarks than those built by human hands. Unseen warriors hover around her battlements—and the banner over her shall float triumphantly amid the chaos of a crumbling world. There is also a Mount Zion in heaven, covered with harpers, and the redeemed in their white vestures are there, and the song they sing has no dying cadence. Its top is crowned with a more glorious temple that ever adorned an earthly city, and there nothing that "can hurt or make afraid" shall ever enter

WHAT strange contrasts this earth of ours presents. It seems to be the middle spot between heaven and hell, and to partake of the character of both. Beings from both are found moving over its surface, and scenes from both are constantly occurring upon it. The glory from one and the midnight shades from the other meet along its bosom, and the song of angels and the shriek of fiends go up from the same spot. Noonday and midnight are not more opposite than the scenes that are constantly passing before our eyes. The temple of God stands beside a brothel, and the place of prayer is separated only by a dwelling from the "hell" of the gam-

Harding. Burt.

MOUNT TABOR.

bler. Truth and falsehood walk side by side through our streets, and vice and virtue meet and pass every hour of the day. The hut of the starving stands in the shadow of the palace of the wealthy, and the carriage of Dives every day throws the dust of its glittering wheels over the tattered garments of Lazarus. Health and sickness lie down in the same apartment; joy and agony look out of the same window; and hope and despair dwell under the same roof. The cry of the new-born infant and the groan of the dying rise together from the same dwelling; the funeral procession treads close on the heels of the bridal party, and the tones of the lute and viol have scarcely died away before the requiem for the dead comes swelling after. Oh! the beautiful and deformed, the pure and corrupt, joy and sorrow, ecstacies and agonies, life and death, are strangely blent on this restless planet of ours.

But the past and future present as strange contrasts as the present. What different events have transpired on the same spot. Where the smoke of the Indian's wigwam arose, and the stealthy tread of the wolf and panther was heard over the autumn leaves at twilight, the population of New York now surges along. Where once Tyre the queen of the sea stood, fishermen are spreading their nets on the desolate rocks, and the bright waves are rolling over its marble columns. In the empty apartments of Edom the fox makes his den, and the dust of the desert is sifting over the forsaken ruins of Palmyra. The owl hoots in the ancient halls of kings, and the wind of the summer night makes sad music through the rents of once gorgeous palaces. The Arab spurs his steed along the streets of ancient Jerusalem, or scornfully stands and curls his lip at the pilgrim pressing wearily to the sepulchre of the Saviour. The Muezzin's voice rings over the bones of the prophets, and the desert wind heaps the dust above the foundations of the seven churches of Asia. Oh, now good and evil, light and darkness, chase each other over the world.

Forty-seven years ago, a form was seen standing on Mount Tabor with which the world has since become familiar. It was a bright spring morning, and as he sat on his steed in the clear sunlight, his eye rested on a scene in the vale below, which was sublime and appalling enough to quicken the pulsations of the calmest heart. That form was Napoleon Bonaparte, and the scene before him the fierce and terrible "BATTLE OF MOUNT TABOR." From Nazareth, where the Saviour once trod, Kleber had marched with three thousand French soldiers forth into the plain, when lo, at the foot of Mount Tabor he saw the whole Turkish army drawn up in order of battle. Fifteen thousand infantry and twelve thousand splendid cavalry moved down in majestic strength on this band of three thousand French. Kleber had scarcely time to throw his handful of men into squares, with the cannon at the angles, before those twelve thousand horse, making the earth smoke and thunder as they came, burst in a headlong gallop upon them. But round those steady squares rolled a fierce devouring fire, emptying the saddles of those wild horsemen with frightful rapidity, and strewing the earth with the bodies of riders and steeds together Again and again did those splendid squadrons wheel, re-form and charge with deafening shouts, while their uplifted and flashing scimitars gleamed like a forest of steel through the smoke of battle: but that same wasting fire received them; till those squares seemed bound by a girdle of flame, so rapid and constant were the discharges. Before their certain and deadly aim, as they stood fighting for existence, the charging squadrons fell so fast that a rampart of dead bodies was soon formed around them. Behind this embankment of dead men and horses this band of warriors stood and fought for six dreadful hours, and was still steadily thinning the ranks of the enemy, when Napoleon debouched with a single division on Mount Tabor, and turned his eye below. What a scene met his gaze. The whole plain was filled with marching columns and charging squadrons of wildly galloping steeds, while the thunder of cannon and fierce rattle of musketry, amid which now and then was heard the blast of thousands of trumpets, and strains of martial music, filled all the air. The smoke of battle was rolling furiously over the hosts, and all was confusion and chaos in his sight. Amid the twenty-seven thousand Turks that crowded the plain and enveloped their enemy like a cloud, and amid the incessant discharge of artillery and musketry, Napoleon could tell where his own brave troops were struggling, only by the steady simultaneous vollies which showed how discipline was contending with the wild valor of overpowering numbers. The constant flashes from behind that rampart of dead bodies were like spots of flame on the tumultuous and chaotic field. Napoleon descended from Mount Tabor with his little band, while a single twelve-pounder, fired from the heights, told the wearied Kleber that he was rushing to the rescue. Then for the first time he took the offensive, and pouring his enthusiastic followers on the foe, carried death and terror over the field. Thrown into confusion, and trampled under foot, that mighty army rolled turbulently back towards the Jordan, where Murat was anxiously waiting to mingle in the fight. Dashing with his cavalry among the disordered ranks, he sabred them down without mercy, and raged like a lion amid the prey. This chivalric and romantic warrior declared that the remembrance of the scenes that once transpired on Mount Tabor, and on these thrice consecrated spots, came to him in the hottest of the fight, and nerved him with tenfold courage.

As the sun went down over the plains of Palestine, and twilight shed its dim ray over the rent and trodden and dead-covered field, a sulphurous cloud hung around the summit of Mount Tabor. The smoke of battle had settled there where once the cloud of glory rested, while groans and shrieks and cries rent the air. Nazareth, Jordan and Mount Tabor! what spots for battle-fields!

Roll back twenty centuries and again view that hill. The day is bright and beautiful as then, and the same rich oriental landscape is smiling in the same sun. There is Nazareth with its busy population,—the same Nazareth from which Kleber marched his army: and there is Jordan rolling its bright waters along,—the same Jordan along whose banks charged the glittering squadrons of Murat's cavalry: and there is Mount Tabor,—the same on which Bonaparte stood with his cannon: and the same beautiful plain where rolled the smoke of battle, and struggled thirty thousand men in mortal combat. But how different is the scene that is passing there. The Son of God stands on that height and casts his eye over the quiet valley through which Jordan winds its silver current. Three friends are beside Him: they have walked together up the toilsome way, and now the four stand, mere specks on the distant summit. Far away to the northwest shines the blue Mediterranean—all around is the great plain of Esdraelon and Galilee—eastward, the lake of Tiberias dots the landscape, while Mount Carmel lifts its naked summit in the distance. But the glorious landscape at their feet is forgotten in a sublimer scene that is passing before them. The son of Mary—the carpenter of Nazareth—the wanderer with whom they have ate and drank and travelled on foot many a weary league, in all the intimacy of companions and friends, begins to change before their eyes. Over his soiled and coarse garments is spreading a strange light, steadily brightening into intenser beauty, till that form glows with such splendor that it seems to waver to and fro and dissolve in the still radiance.

The three astonished friends gaze on it in speechless admiration, then turn to that familiar face. But lo, a greater change has passed over it. The man has put on the God, and that sad and solemn countenance which has been so often seen stooping over the couch of the dying, and entering the door of the hut of poverty, and passing through the streets of Jerusalem, and pausing by the weary wayside—aye, bedewed with the tears of pity,—now burns like the sun in his midday splendor. Meekness has given way to majesty—sadness to dazzling glory—the look of pity to the grandeur of a God. The still radiance of heaven sits on that serene brow, and all around that divine form flows an atmosphere of strange and wondrous beauty. Heaven has poured its brightness over that consecrated spot, and on the beams of light which glitter there, Moses and Elias have descended; and, wrapped in the same shining vestments, stand beside him. Wonder follows wonder, for those three glittering forms are talking with each other, and amid the thrilling accents are heard the words "Mount Olivet," "Calvary," the agony and the death of the crucifixion. Peter, awe-struck and overcome, feeling also the influence of that heavenly atmosphere, and carried away by a sudden impulse, says to Jesus, in low and tremulous accents: "It is good to be here; let us build three tabernacles; one for thee, one for Moses, and one for Elias." Confused by the scene and dazzled by the splendor, he was ignorant what he was saying. He knew not the meaning of this sudden appearance, but he knew that heaven was near and God revealing himself, and he felt that some sacred ceremony would be appropriate to the scene; and while his bewildered gaze was fixed on the three forms before him, his unconscious lips murmured forth the feelings of his heart. No wonder a sudden fear came over him, that paralyzed his tongue and crushed him to the earth, when in the midst of his speech he saw a cloud fall like a falling star from heaven, and, bright and dazzling, balance itself over those forms of light. Perhaps his indiscreet interruption had brought this new messenger down, and from its bosom the thunder and flame of Sinai were to burst; and he fell on his face in silent terror. But that cloud was only a canopy for its God, and from its bright foldings came a voice, saying, "This is my beloved Son, in whom I am well pleased, hear ye Him."

How long the vision lasted we cannot tell, but all that night did Jesus, with his friends, stay on that lonely mountain. Of the conversation that passed between them there we know nothing: but little sleep, we imagine, visited their eyes that night; and as they sat on the high summit and watched the stars, as they rose one after another above the horizon, and gazed on the moon as she poured her light over the dim and darkened landscape, words were spoken that seemed born of heaven and truths never to be forgotten were uttered in the ears of the subdued and reverent disciples.

Oh, how different is heaven and earth! Can there be a stranger contrast than the Battle and Transfiguration of Mount Tabor? One shudders to think of Bonaparte and the Son of God on the same mountain: one with his wasting cannon by his side, and the other with Moses and Elias just from heaven.

But no after desecration can destroy the first consecration of Mount Tabor; for, baptized with the glory of heaven, and honored with the wondrous scene of the Transfiguration, it stands a *Sacred Mountain* on the earth.

Harding. Burt.

MOUNT OF OLIVES.

THE Mount of Olives stands just without Jerusalem, over the little stream of Kedron. Its height and magnitude would not entitle it to the name of mountain as we use the word; but being called such in the Bible, it belongs among the "Sacred Mountains." In *moral* grandeur it towers above all the preceding summits that rise along the horizon of history.

It is difficult to recall any scene vividly that has been so often described and so long familiar to us as that which transpired on the Mount of Olives. The mind is prepared for every event in it, and hence cannot be taken by surprise or held in suspense. But there *are* moments when the heart forgets all that it has ever heard, and seems for the first time to witness that night of suffering. The indifference which long familiarity has produced, disappears before rising emotion, and that lonely hill-top—that midnight prayer—that piercing agony, with its bloody testimonial, and the rude shock of Roman soldiers, all, all, swim before the swimming eye, with the freshness of first sight, till the heart thrills and throbs at the solemn spectacle.

But morally grand and moving as that scene was, it caused but little talk in Jerusalem. The streets of the proud city were filled with careless promenaders—parties of pleasure were assembled—dissipation and revelry were on every side; and the quiet of the staid citizen's home was not interrupted by the tragedy Mount Olivet was to witness. Every thing moved on in its accustomed way, when, in an obscure street, in the upper chamber of an inferior dwelling, a group of coarse-clad men sat down to a table spread with the plainest fare. The rattling of carriages and the hum of the mighty city were unheeded by them, and you could see by their countenances that some calamity was impending over their heads. Few words were spoken, and those few were uttered in a subdued and saddened tone, that always bespeaks grief at the heart. At the head of the table sat one whose noble countenance proclaimed him chief there. He had won the love of those simple-hearted men, and now they sat grouped around him, expecting some sad news; but oh, they were unprepared for the startling declaration that fell from those lips: "*This night one of you shall betray me.*" "*Is it I?*" "*Is it I?*" ran from lip to lip in breathless consternation. At length all eyes centred on Judas, and he rose and went away.

I will not speak of the conversation that followed; but amid words that thrilled every heart was heard such language as, "*This is my blood shed for many;*" and as the bread crumbled beneath his fingers, "*This is my body;*"—strange language, and awakening strange sensations in the bewildered listeners; and a mournful sadness rested on every face, as through the silent chamber rung those tones of tenderness.

Gradually the great city sunk to rest, the noise of wheels grew less and less, and only now and then a solitary carriage went rumbling by. It was midnight, and from that solitary chamber arose the voice of singing. The victim at the altar—the sufferer by the wheel, struck up a hymn at the moment of sacrifice. Was there ever before a hymn sung under such circumstances?

Through the darkened streets those twelve forms are slowly passing towards the walls of the city, cared for and noticed only by the police, whom the betrayer has put upon the track. Kedron is passed, and they reach the garden of Gethsemane. "Sit you here," says Jesus, "while I go and pray yonder," and taking with him only Peter and James and

John, he ascended the slope of Olivet. As they paused on the solitary summit, the human heart threw off the restraint it had put on its feelings, and burst forth in tones of indescribable mournfulness, "*My soul is exceeding sorrowful, even unto death; stay here and watch with me.*" Every prop seemed falling beside him, and in the deepening gloom and dread that surrounded him, he reached out for sympathy and aid. Then, as if recollecting himself and the task before him, he broke away even from those three remaining friends, and they saw with speechless grief and amazement his form disappear in the darkness.

Jerusalem is sunk in slumber and security, and naught but the tread of the watchman is heard along the streets. The disciples in the garden of Gethsemane are quietly sleeping below, and all is still and solemn, as night ever is when left alone; and the large luminous stars are shining down in their wonted beauty. Kedron goes murmuring by as if singing in its dreams, and the olive trees rustle to the passing breeze as if their leaves were but half stirred from their slumbers. It is night, most quiet night, with all its accompaniments of beauty and of loveliness.

But hark, from the summit of Mount Olivet, rises a low and plaintive moan; and there stretched on the dewy grass, his face to the earth, are seen the dim outlines of a human form. All is still around, save that moan which rises in a deep perpetual monotone, like the last cry of helpless suffering. But listen again; a prayer is ascending the heavens: and what a prayer, and in what tones it is uttered. Such accents never before rung on the ear of God or man: "*Father, if it be possible, let this cup pass from me.*" It is still again, and nature herself seems to gasp for breath; and lo, there arises another voice in tones of resignation sweeter than angels use, "*Father, not my will but thine be done.*" Oh, what inexpressible tenderness is poured in that word "*Father*"—the very passion and soul of love is breathed forth in it. Wearied and worn, that tottering form slowly rises and moves through the gloom towards where the three friends are sleeping—going in its humanity after sympathy. The pressure is too great—the sorrow and despair too deep, and the human heart reaches out imploringly for help. "*What, could you not watch with me one hour?*" falls on their slumberous ears, and the lonely sufferer turns again to his solitude and his woe. Prone on the earth he again casts himself, and the wave comes back with a heavier and a darker flow. Bursting sighs, and groans that rend the heart again startle the midnight air, and down those pale cheeks the blood is trickling, and the dewy grass turns red, as if a wounded man were weltering there. The life-stream is flowing from the crushed heart, as it trembles and wrestles in the grasp of its mighty agony. Woe and darkness, and horror inconceivable, indescribable, gather in fearful companionship around that prostrate form, but still the prayer goes up, and still the voice of resignation hovers amid the tumult like the breath of God over a world in chaos,—ruling the wild scene.

Oh, is this the form that a few days ago stood on this same height and looked off on Jerusalem sleeping below, while the sunlight around, and the fragrant breezes loaded with the scent of the pomegranate and vine, visited in kindness his brow, and the garden smiled up in his face from beneath, and garments were strewed before him, and branches of palm waved around him, and "HOSANNA TO THE HIGHEST!" shook the hill? Alas, what a change has passed over him! No hosannas greet his ear, but deep within his soul are voices of terror and dismay, striving, but in vain, to shake his constancy or darken his faith.

Christ arose from the earth he had moistened with his blood, and stood beneath the stars, that still shone on as tranquilly as if all unconscious of the scene that had transpired in their light. Kedron still murmured by, and the night air stirred the leaves as gently as ever. All was sweet and tranquil, when torches were seen dancing to and fro along the slopes of the hill, and the heavy tread of approaching feet was heard, and rough voices broke the holy quiet of nature; and soon Roman helmets flashed through the gloom, and swords glittered in the torch-light, and a band of soldiers drew up before the "man of sorrows." "*Whom seek ye?*" fell in languid and quiet accents on their ears "Jesus of Nazareth," was the short and stern reply. "*I am he,*" answered them, but in tones that had more of God than man in them, for swords and torches sunk to the earth at their utterance, and those mailed warriors staggered back and fell like dead men. It was not the haggard and blood-streaked face over which the torches shed their sudden glare, that unnerved them so;

for they were used to scenes of violence and of murder—it was the God speaking from the man.

"But so it must be, that the Scriptures may be fulfilled;" and the betrayer and his accomplices take up their fallen weapons, and freed from the sudden awe that overwhelmed them, close threateningly around their unresisting victim. With their prisoner they clatter down the declivity of Olivet, cross Kedron, and soon their heavy tread resounds along the streets of Jerusalem as they hurry on to the house of the high priest. Why speak of the painful desertion of his followers, sufficient of itself to break a noble heart—of the rude treatment of the brutal officers that guarded him, or of the mockery of a trial, destitute even of the forms of justice! Why speak of Peter's treachery, rebuked only by a sorrowful look; or of all or any of the shameful proceedings that made this last most terrible night of the Son of God a fit prelude to the crowning act of human wickedness!

The night wanes away—the morning, the last dreadful morning approaches, and the scenes of Mount Olivet are to disappear before the fearful tragedy of Mount Calvary.

Mount Calvary is lord of the "Sacred Mountains," and by its baptism of blood and agony, its moral grandeur, and the intense glory that beams from its summit, is worthy to crown the immortal group. Its moral height no man can measure, for though its base is on the earth, its top is lost in the heaven of heavens. The angels hover around the dazzling summit, struggling in vain to scale its highest point, which has never yet been fanned by even an immortal wing. The Divine eye alone embraces its length and breadth, and depth and heighth.

What associations cluster around Mount Calvary! what mysteries hover there, and what revelations it makes to the awe-struck beholder! Mount Calvary! at the mention of that name the universe thrills with a new emotion, and heaven trembles with a new anthem, in which pity and exultation mingle in strange, yet sweet accord. Glory and brightness are on that hill-top, and shall be to the end of time; but there was a morning when gloom and terror crowned it, and heaven itself, all but God the Father, gazed on it in wonder, if not in consternation.

The strange and painful scene in the garden had passed by, and the shameful examination in the lighted chamber of the high priest was over. Insult and contempt had marked every step of the villainous proceedings, till at length one wretch more impious than the rest advanced and struck Christ in the face. The cheek reddened to the blow, but not with anger or shame; yet methinks as the sound of that buffet was borne on high, there was a rustling of myriad wings, as angels started from their listening attitude, waiting the thunderbolt that should follow.

This too passed by, and also the second mockery of a trial in Pilate's hall; and the uprisen sun was flashing down on the towers and domes of Jerusalem, and the vast population was again abroad, thronging every street. But a few took any interest in the fate of Jesus of Nazareth, yet those few were filled with the bitterest hate. The victim was now in their power—given up to their will, and they commenced the bloody scene they were to enact, by spitting in his face and striking his unresisting cheek with blow after blow. To give greater force to their insults, they put a crown on his head, made of thorns, and mocked him with sarcastic words, and strove with fiendish skill to irritate him into some sign of anger or complaint. After having exhausted their ingenuity, and failing in every endeavor, they "led him away to be crucified."

It was a bright and beautiful day when a

train passed out of the gates of Jerusalem, and began to ascend the slope of Mount Calvary. The people paused a moment as the procession moved boisterously along the streets, then making some careless remark about the fate of fanatics, passed on. The low and base of both sexes turned and joined the company, and with jokes and laughter hurried on to the scene of excitement. Oh, how unsympathizing did nature seem: the vine and fig-tree shed their fragrance around —the breeze whispered nothing but love and tranquillity, while the blue and bending arch above seemed delighted with the beauty and verdure the spread-out earth presented. The birds were singing in the gardens, all reckless of the roar and jar of the great city near, as Jesus passed by in the midst of the mob. His face was colorless as marble, save where the blood trickled down his cheeks from the thorns that pierced his temples; his knees trembled beneath him, though not with fear, and he staggered on under the heavy timber that weighed him down, till at last he fainted. Nature gave way, and he sunk to the earth, while the hue of death passed over his countenance. When the sudden rush around him, caused by his fall, had subsided, the cross, or rather *cross-piece*, which he had carried was given to another, and the procession again took up the line of march. But suddenly, over the confused noise of the throng and rude shouts of the mob, there came a wild lament. Friends were following after, whose sick, Christ had healed, whose wounded hearts he had bound up, and on whose pathway of darkness he had shed the light of heaven; and now they lifted up their voices in one long, mournful cry. He turned at the sound and listened a moment, then murmured in mournful accents: "*Weep not for me, but weep for yourselves and your children.*" Jerusalem on fire suddenly rose on his vision, together with its famine-struck and bloated population, staggering and dying around the empty market-places—the heaps of the dead that loaded the air with pestilence, and all the horror and woe and carnage of that last dreadful siege; and forgetful of his own suffering, he exclaimed, "*Weep not for me, but for yourselves and your children.*"

Soon the procession reached the hill-top, and Christ was laid upon the ground, and his arms stretched along the timber he had carried, with the palms upturned, and through them spikes driven, fastening them to the wood. Methinks I hear the strokes of the hammer as it sends the iron, with blow after blow, through the quivering tendons, and behold the painful workings of that agony-wrung brow, and the convulsive heaving and swelling of that blessed bosom, which seemed striving to rend above the imprisoned heart.

At length he is lifted from the ground—his weight dragging on the spikes through his hands; and the cross-piece inserted into the mortice of the upright timber, and a heavy iron crushed through his feet, fastening them to the main post, and he is left to die. Why speak of his agony—of his words of comfort to the dying thief—of the multitude around him, or of the disgrace of that death. Not even to look on that pallid face and flowing blood could one get any conception of the suffering of the victim. The gloom and terror that began to gather round the *soul*, as every aid, human and divine, withdrew itself, and it stood alone in the deserted, darkened universe, and shuddered, was all unseen by mortal eye. Yet even in this dreadful hour his benevolent heart did not forget its friends. Looking down from the cross, he saw the mother that bore him gazing in tears upon his face, and with a feeble and tremulous voice, he turned to John, who had so often lain in his bosom, and said, "Son, behold thy mother." Then turning to his mother, he said, "*Behold thy son.*" His business with earthly things was now over, and he summoned his energies to meet the last most terrible blow, before which nature itself was to give way. He had hitherto endured all without a complaint—the mocking, the spitting upon, the cross, the nails and the agony—but now came a woe that broke his heart. *His father's—his own father's frown began to darken upon him.* Oh! who can tell the anguish of that loving, trusting, abandoned heart at the sight. It was too much, and there arose a cry so piercing and shrill and wild that the universe shivered before it; and as the accents, "*My God, my God, why hast* THOU *forsaken me?*" fell on the ears of astonished mortals, and filled heaven with alarm; the earth gave a groan, as if she too was about to expire; the sun died in the heavens; an earthquake thundered on to complete the dismay; and the dead could no longer sleep, but burst their ghastly cerements, and came forth to look upon the scene. That was the gloomiest wave that ever broke over the soul of the Saviour, and he fell before it. *Christ was dead:* and to all human appearance, the world was an orphan.

How heaven regarded this disaster, and the universe felt at the sight, I cannot tell. I know not but tears fell like rain-drops from angelic eyes, when they saw Christ spit upon and struck. I know not but there was silence on high for *more* than "half an hour," when the scene of the crucifixion was transpiring—a silence unbroken, save by the solitary sound of some harp-string on which unconsciously fell the agitated, trembling fingers of a seraph. I know not but all the radiant ranks on high, and even Gabriel himself turned with the deepest solicitude to the Father's face, to see if he was calm and untroubled amid it all. I know not but his composed brow and serene majesty were all that restrained heaven from one universal shriek of horror, when they heard groans on Calvary, *dying* groans. I know not but they thought God had "given his glory to another;" but one thing I do know—that when they saw through the vast design, comprehended the stupendous scheme, the hills of God shook to a shout that had never before rung over their bright tops, and the crystal sea trembled to a song that had never before stirred its bright depths, and the "GLORY TO GOD IN THE HIGHEST," was a "sevenfold chorus of hallelujahs and harping symphonies."

Yet none of the heavenly cadences reached the earth, and all was sad, dark and despairing around Mount Calvary. The excitement which the slow murder had created, vanished. With none to resist, and none to be slain, a change came over the feelings of the multitude, and they began one by one to return to the city. The sudden darkness also, that wrapped the heavens, and the throb of the earthquake, which made those three crosses reel to and fro like cedars in a tempest, had sobered their feelings, and all but the soldiery were glad to be away from a scene that had ended with such supernatural exhibitions. Gradually the noise and confusion around the cross receded down the slopes—the shades of evening began to creep over the landscape, throwing into still more ghastly relief those three white corpses stretched on high and streaked with blood—and all was over. No! *not* over, for the sepulchre was yet to open, and the slain Christ was yet to mount the heavens in his glorious ascension.

I will not speak of the moral grandeur of the atonement—of the redemption purchased by the agony and death on Calvary, for they are familiar to all. Still they constitute the greatness and value of the whole. It is the atonement that makes Mount Calvary chief among the "Sacred Mountains"—gives it such altitude that no mortal eye can scan its top, or bear the full effulgence of its glory. Paul called on his young disciples to summon their strongest energies and bend their highest efforts to comprehend the "length and breadth, and depth and height" of this stupendous theme—"a length which reaches from everlasting to everlasting; a breadth that encompasses every intelligence and every interest; a depth which reaches the lowest state of human degradation and misery, and *a height that throws floods of glory on the throne and crown of Jehovah.*"

In the preceding sketches I have confined myself to descriptions of scenes alone, not because there was no great moral truth inculcated in them, but to give them definiteness. Each is full of instruction, and indeed was designed to be a great lesson for man. Sometimes God's hatred of sin, sometimes his care for his children, sometimes the discipline of his church, were the motives that led him to make such wonderful displays of his power, his terror, and his goodness. But besides their present benefit, they have also an ultimate meaning; and those immortal mountains, with their silent yet eloquent summits, all point to a spiritual elevation, whose top is lost in the glorious atmosphere of the upper world. Thus Ararat, with the heaven-lifted, heaven-guided ark resting on its summit, is but a symbol of the Christian's repose, after the storms of life, and wreck of all earthly things, on the serene heights of perpetual bliss. Mount Moriah is only the shadow of that height of mystery where God offered up his only son, and there was no hand to stay the stroke. Sinai and Horeb are but dim reflections of the terrors of that law whose final execution shall set the world in a blaze. Mount Pisgah points to a "land of promise," from whose bosom rise more glorious summits than the "goodly mountain Lebanon." Tabor reveals beforehand the appearance which the Lamb of God will present when he stands on "Mount Zion" with the redeemed about him; and Olivet and Calvary are both eloquent of heaven. All these, as I remarked, point more or less significantly to one transcendent mountain, whose summit has never been seen but once from earth. There is one mount whose dazzling outline is hid from human eye by impenetrable veils of glory. The Bible often speaks of the "Mount of God," the "Mount of Holiness," and "Mount Zion"—sometimes referring to Horeb and sometimes to the heights of Jerusalem, and sometimes to the moral and spiritual heights of paradise. To represent these last I have chosen the title of "Mount of God."

In that strange era in human history when God walked with man, clad *as* a man, and earth was nearer to heaven than ever before, amid the few friends that clustered around him, was *one "disciple whom Jesus loved."* Of a warm and devoted heart, John had allowed his attachment to absorb every other feeling of his nature, and he merged his life into that of the Saviour. He accompanied his footsteps as he walked, looked up into his face with unutterable tenderness as he spoke, and lay in his bosom as he sat at meat. No wonder that in the days of persecution the hand of violence should fall on such a man. Proscribed, banished—the solitary inhabitant of Patmos—John passed his days in musing on the words and fate of his departed Lord. But one morning—the morning that brought to remembrance his glorious ascension—he was "in the spirit," and that lonely isle "became like Carmel of old filled with horses and chariots of fire." He "*was in the spirit*," and there was nothing to disturb his high and holy meditations. There was no sound of passing wheels, no hum of distant voices, no tread of hurried footsteps, to break the solitude that surrounded him. The only sound that fell on his ear, as he trode the solitary shore, was the deep and solemn murmur of the Egean sea, as it gently rolled its waves to his feet. As he thus passed along, wrapped in his solitary musings, he suddenly heard behind him a voice like the solemn peal of a mighty trumpet, saying, "I AM ALPHA AND OMEGA, THE FIRST AND THE LAST." And as he turned and beheld the form which spake to him, he was filled with awe and consternation, and "fell on his face as a dead man." Before those burning footsteps those eyes of flame, and voice like the sound of many waters, that countenance shining like the sun in his mid-day splendor, he sunk powerless and affrighted, and buried his face in the sand and lay speechless till he felt the pressure of "his right hand" upon him, and heard the cheering words, "Fear not, I am the first and the last; I am he that was dead, and is alive forevermore." Then followed a succession of wonderful revelations, till at length the heavens were opened above him, and he saw the throne and him that sat upon it, circled by the emerald rainbow, surrounded by the white-vested elders, while all around and far away into eternity unceasingly rose and fell, "Holy, holy, holy, Lord God Almighty, which was, and is, and is to come." Thus vision after vision passed before his bewildered, trembling spirit, till he stood and wept amid the awful pageantry of heaven. At last, to crown the scene, a mount rose before him bathed in an atmosphere all its own, and on its dazzling top stood the still more dazzling form of the Lamb, in more than earthly transfiguration, and beside him a hundred and forty four thousand resplendent beings, with the Father's name written in strange but heavenly characters on their foreheads. The crystal sea laved the base of that mountain, and from its top the "river of God" was seen rolling its bright waters along, and the heavenly Jerusalem, with its walls of jasper and gates of pearl, standing open night and day, and its temple of light. As the bewildered disciple stood gazing on this wonderful vision, suddenly there stole on his ears strains of music. At first faint and low the thrilling accents rose from that mysterious mount, then swelled triumphantly away, till the universe was filled with the melody. The singers were those hundred and forty four thousand, and they sung a *new song*, and as they struck their harps, together thus they sung: "Worthy is the Lamb that was slain, to receive power, and riches, and wisdom, and strength, and honor, and glory, and blessing." And with one voice the innumerable host chanted the heavenly doxology, "Blessing, and honor, and glory, and power, be unto him that sitteth on the throne, and to the Lamb forever;" and back returned the long "Amen." Again and again was it taken up and echoed from rank to rank along that celestial mountain, till it came rolling back with all the strength of archangel voices full on the throne of God. The theme, the song was new—it was the song of Redemption. David stood there sweeping a harp far more melodious and tuneful than the one he swept with such a master hand on earth. Elijah poured his soul of fire into it. Isaiah gave it a loftier echo. The martyrs, those witnesses for the truth who had passed through the flames to their reward, furnished new accessions to its strength, for all the ransomed of the Lord were there. Aaron went up thither from the top of Hor, and Moses from Pisgah. Elijah's chariot of fire never stopped till its burning wheels rested on that heavenly mount, and thither Christ ascended from the hill of Olives. Thus the redeemed have flocked one after another to the Mount of God, and there they shall continue to gather until the glorious assembly stands complete. and "God is all and in all."

THE END.

www.ingramcontent.com/pod-product-compliance
Lightning Source LLC
LaVergne TN
LVHW011220110826
845150LV00006B/1489

9781425516666